The Michigan
Business Activities Tax

The Michigan
Business Activities Tax

Value-Added Taxation in
the Subnational Economy

Robert D. Ebel

Economic Research Center
University of Hawaii

1972
MSU Business Studies
Division of Research
Graduate School of Business Administration
Michigan State University
East Lansing

ISBN: 0-87744-110-3
Library of Congress Catalog Card Number: 71-189476
© 1972 by The Board of Trustees of Michigan State University
East Lansing, Michigan. All rights reserved
Printed in the United States of America

To Dorothy and Paul

Contents

List of Tables

Preface

The author is indebted to many people who made contributions to the book. Michigan data collection was facilitated by the cooperation and professionalism of the staff of the Revenue Division of the Michigan Department of Treasury, especially Clarence W. Lock and C. Harold Knudstrup. In addition, many constructive comments and criticisms were made by Professors James Mak of the University of Hawaii; Jay W. Wiley and George Horwich of Purdue University; and Professor Kenneth R. Biederman of Georgetown University. Claire M. Toner, economic consultant to the State of Hawaii, read the manuscript several times and made many substantive suggestions on all versions of the study.

Special mention must go to James A. Papke of Purdue whose suggestions, advice, and judgment on state tax matters are invaluable. Professor Papke gave much of his time and ideas to the author, especially at the crucial early stages of the book. Finally, a debt is owed to Jean Taga, Karen Higa, and Gail Sugano who typed the original manuscript, and to Elizabeth Marcus of Michigan State University whose thorough editing made the book suitable for publication.

The study was financed by grants from the Herman C. Krannert Graduate School of Industrial Administration at Purdue University and the Economic Research Center of the University of Hawaii.

Of course, any errors and omissions in the book are solely the fault of my wife.

15

1

Introduction

Throughout the postwar years state governments have been caught in a financial squeeze. States have assumed an increasing fiscal responsibility for nondefense programs such as education, highways, welfare, and health.[1] Expanding requirements and rising costs have pushed expenditures for public services upward at a more rapid rate than state income. Yet, given the conventional distribution of revenue sources and fiscal control between state, local, and federal government, subnational units have been forced to rely on taxes which will not automatically generate revenues to meet future spending needs. Moreover, these discrepancies are likely to continue. Projections of future spending by subnational governments indicate that revenues from existing sources will grow only half as rapidly as expenditure commitments.[2]

1. U.S. Department of Commerce, Bureau of the Census, *Historical Statistics of the United States: Colonial Times to 1957* (Washington, D.C.: U.S. Government Printing Office, 1960), Series Y401-411, 547-574, 670-682; U.S. Department of Commerce, Bureau of the Census, *Government Finances in 1965–66* (Washington, D.C.: U.S. Government Printing Office, 1967), pp. 22–25.

2. L. L. Ecker-Racz, "Emerging Fiscal Issues: Roundup of the Seminar," in *Proceedings of the Seminar on Balancing Our Federal-State-Local Fiscal System* (Columbus: National Tax Association, 1971), p. 421.

During the past decade, revenues of subnational governments have been derived mainly from increased tax rates or from new taxes on individuals either as consumers, income recipients, or wealth holders (for example, retail sales taxes, personal income taxes, and property taxes respectively).[3] That a further reliance on such taxes is desirable or, indeed, even possible is questionable; but that the business and industrial sectors will have to share in the fiscal responsibilities accompanying increasing public service demands on subnational governments seems inevitable.

Within this context there are several critical questions. Can existing state government revenue sources support continued rate increases? If these conventional sources are relied upon more intensively, will their structural defects become more pronounced? In view of the growing national–subnational fiscal mismatch, will it become necessary for states to relinquish some of their fiscal autonomy to the federal government? Or, are there other tax measures which are available, but which have not yet been sufficiently explored? If so, to what extent do these taxes succeed or fail in achieving various normative objectives of state tax policy?

In response to these questions, this book examines in detail the background, statutory provisions, and structural and economic characteristics of the Michigan Business Activities Tax (BAT). Enacted by the Michigan Legislature in 1953 and repealed in 1968, the tax is perhaps the only genuine innovation in state business taxation since the adoption of the corporate net income levy by Wisconsin in 1911. The Michigan BAT is the first and thus far the only use by a governmental unit in the United States of a general business tax on value added (the net dollar value contributed by the business enterprise to the output of goods and services in the state). Although substantial publicity has been given to value-added taxation at the national level, little attention has been given to its use by subnational governments.[4]

---

3. Advisory Commission on Intergovernmental Relations, *Fiscal Balance in the American Federal System*, Report A-31, vol. 1 (Washington, D.C.: U.S. Government Printing Office, 1967), pp. 116–17.

4. For a review of various proposals for use of value-added taxation by national and subnational governments in the United States see John F. Due, "Value Added Tax Proposals in the United States," in *Public Finance and Welfare: Essays in Honor of C. Ward Macy*, edited by Paul L. Kleinsorge (Eugene: University of Oregon Press, 1966), pp. 111–26; and Richard W. Lindholm, "The Value Added Tax: A Short Review of the Literature," *Journal of Economic Literature* 8 (December 1970): 1178–89.

The purpose of this study is twofold. First, the Michigan experience provides the only empirical opportunity to analyze and evaluate the suitability of the value-added tax as a form of state business taxation. Those responsible for formulating future state tax policy must be provided information as to the nature of the BAT, its merits and defects, and the effect which specific legislative provisions had on the BAT's achievement of various normative objectives of state business taxation. Second, given the pressures on state governments for additional revenues, increased competition for the location of industry, and demands for tax reform, the Business Activities Tax may well be the forerunner of future developments in state–local business tax policy. Indeed, since 1965 the value-added tax has been recommended for consideration in New York City, California, Indiana, Iowa, Hawaii, Texas, West Virginia, and again in Michigan.

Specifically, the BAT is examined within the context of neutrality or equity among the different factor inputs, tax impact on various business classifications, comprehensiveness of coverage in terms of total state business activity, responsiveness to state economic growth, certainty of shifting, ease of administration and taxpayer compliance, and effects on state industrial location and growth. In addition, the question of state revenue collection and interindustry tax liability effects of alternative allocation formulas for multistate business receipts is empirically examined.

Congressional proposals are made periodically to provide a uniform method for interstate apportionment of tax bases of businesses operating in interstate commerce. Because the issue of apportionment is of crucial importance to the revenue productivity of any state income or value-added tax base, calculations from Michigan BAT returns on an industry-by-industry basis are provided to illustrate the tax liability effects of various multistate apportionment proposals.

Thus, although this book focuses on a state business tax which no longer exists, the analysis is not an historical account of an old tax. On the contrary, the issues examined and their policy implications are of current and future importance.

2

Fiscal and

Legislative Background

Until the early 1930s, Michigan, as did most states, relied primarily on property and miscellaneous excise and selective tax levies for revenue. In 1932, more than 80 percent of the state's tax money was derived from highway user and property taxes.[1] At the same time, property values and personal incomes began to fall sharply, and there was political pressure to reduce the personal taxation burden. Consequently, in 1932 Michigan adopted a constitutional amendment which limited the property tax rate. In addition, the state government withdrew completely from the general property tax field in favor of local governmental units.[2] In order to meet and finance demands for state services during the Great Depression, Michigan, along with a dozen other states, enacted a retail sales tax as an emergency revenue measure. The sales tax immediately became the major revenue producer for the state's General Fund.

In the early postwar years, local and state governments were faced with demands for public goods and services sacrificed during the war.

---

1. Michigan Department of Treasury, Revenue Division, *Annual Report* (Lansing: the Department, 1958–59), pp. 49–50.

2. Ibid., pp. 9–11.

In 1945 local governmental units in Michigan requested more than $18 million in state aid. To meet this demand, the state passed an alcoholic beverages excise levy earmarked for direct distribution to local governments, and relinquished its one-third share of receipts from the intangibles tax.[3] Despite this action, increased pressure for state aid to local governments continued, and in 1946 the Michigan electorate passed the sales tax diversion amendment to the Michigan Constitution. The amendment required that one-sixth of the state's sales tax collections be distributed to villages and townships on a per capita basis, one-sixth to school districts on the basis of school enrollments, and that 44.77 percent of total sales tax receipts from the preceding year be allocated to local school aid funds. As a result, only 22 percent of the sales tax — the state's major revenue producer — was available for the state's own budget. Although the sales tax diversion amendment intensified the need for added revenue at the state level, no major tax legislation was enacted until 1953.

In addition to legal constraints of the amendment, there were other important distribution requirements regarding state taxes collected. For example, 97 percent of the intangibles tax was distributed by the state directly to cities, villages, and townships on a population basis, and the entire proceeds from the motor vehicle, motor fuel, and various specific tax levies either were granted directly to local governments or earmarked for disposition other than to the state General Fund.

Table 1 illustrates the extent of the erosion of tax proceeds for General Fund use in fiscal 1951. Of total state tax revenues, more than 70 percent was earmarked for various special purposes, primarily for local government use.[4] This erosion, coupled with the reluctance of the legislature to enact new broad-based levies, depleted the General Fund surplus amassed during the war years. By the end of fiscal 1952, the accumulated deficit had grown to $65.3 million. The urgency of new tax legislation was further indicated by predictions from the Michigan Department of Treasury that at the end of fiscal 1953 the accumulated General Fund deficit would exceed $90 million.[5]

---

3. Ibid.

4. This situation worsened in the following year as the General Fund share of total tax collections fell from the 1951 level of 29.0 percent to 24.7 percent in fiscal 1952 — the year prior to the enactment of the BAT. See Michigan Tax Survey Advisory Committee, *Michigan Tax Survey, 1952* (Detroit: Legislative Interim Tax and Revenue Study Committee, 1952), p. iii.

5. Alan Gornick, *The Michigan Business Receipts Tax — Its Basis and Eco-*

TABLE 1. Tax Collections and Disposition,
in Thousands of Dollars, 1951

Type of tax	Receipts	Distributions*		State share (General Fund)*	
Sales	239,954	167,117	(69.6)	72,837	(30.4)
Use	7,007	—		7,007	(100.0)
Cigarette	23,241	—		23,241	(100.0)
Corporation fee (ACPF)	11,356	—		11,356	(100.0)
Beer and wine	6,975	—		6,975	(100.0)
Chain store	510	—		510	(100.0)
Severance (gas and oil)	853	—		853	(100.0)
Horse racing	3,652	796	(21.8)	2,856	(78.2)
Intangibles	13,801	13,387	(97.0)	414	(3.0)
Specific taxes	34,039	34,039	(100.0)	—	
Motor fuel	50,660	50,660	(100.0)	—	
Motor vehicle	42,199	42,199	(100.0)	—	
Other	1,018	878	(86.2)	141	(13.8)
Total	435,266	309,077	(71.0)	126,189	(29.0)

SOURCE: Adapted from the Michigan Tax Survey Advisory Committee, *Michigan Tax Survey, 1952* (Detroit: Legislative Interim Tax and Revenue Study Committee, 1952), Part I.
*Percentage composition in parentheses.

Alternative Proposals, 1948-1953

In 1948, Governor G. Mennen Williams proposed the adoption of a corporation net income tax levy as a solution to the General Fund deficit. The legislature opposed this approach, and established a Legislative Interim Tax and Revenue Study Committee, commissioned to publish a report on the entire Michigan state revenue structure. The report, *The Michigan Tax Survey*, was released in 1952.[6]

In addition to the usual two solutions for a state financial crisis, reduced expenditures and/or increased taxes, the revenue study committee strongly recommended that the large-scale revenue sharing commitment with local units be reduced. However, in its summary statement on the issue, the committee recognized the political problems involved in finding any short-run solution by a revised revenue distribution plan, and indicated that the only feasible solution appeared to be the increased revenue approach.[7]

nomic Theory, an address by the Tax Counsel and Director of Tax Affairs of the Ford Motor Company (Ann Arbor: University of Michigan Law Institute, 1952), part II.

6. *Michigan Tax Survey, 1952.*

7. Ibid., pp. ix–x.

Accordingly, various revenue proposals were presented during the 1953 legislative session. These included: (1) a bill to levy a gross receipts tax on wholesalers and manufacturers; (2) a group of minor taxes, loophole closures, and amendments to existing statutes (for example, bills to raise the corporation franchise and inheritance taxes, and to levy new taxes on service enterprises such as hotel accommodations); (3) a flat rate net income tax on both individuals and corporations using the federal income tax base; and (4) a 4 percent corporate profits tax. Legislative battles between proponents and opponents of the income tax proposal characterized the 1953 session, and in the final days the Senate Taxation Committee proposed the BAT as a compromise measure. With almost no debate, the statute passed both the house and senate, allegedly before many members had even read it, much less understood it. Finally, although the governor was critical of the measure, he permitted the Business Activities Tax to become law without executive signature.[8]

The original statute levying the BAT specified 15 March 1955 as its expiration date. Consequently, in 1955 the state legislature debated whether to replace the BAT with a corporate net income levy or to continue it with amendments to eliminate its most controversial features. On the expiration date the legislature extended the life of the tax until the end of the calendar year in order to have more time to review these alternatives. The final action, in June 1955, was enactment of a series of amendments (Act 282) which made various statutory changes in the BAT levy and, in addition, eliminated the expiration clause.

Public Education and Acceptance

In spite of public opposition by the governor, criticism from retailers that the tax was discriminatory, and warnings that the law —

8. Much of this information, particularly that on the public's reaction to the tax, is from unpublished Department of Treasury memos and data, and from interviews and correspondence with the tax commissioner's office. The BAT legislative history is discussed briefly in the following sources: Frank Landers, "Michigan's Business Activities Tax," *State Government* 28 (October 1954): 210–15; Clarence W. Lock, "An Administrative History of Michigan's Business Activities Tax," in *Proceedings of the Forty-Eighth Annual Conference on Taxation* (Columbus: National Tax Association, 1955), pp. 20–25; and various issues of the Michigan Department of Treasury, Revenue Division, *Annual Report*.

especially the original multistate allocation formula — would be declared unconstitutional, the tax was favorably received by the public.[9] A number of factors led to its acceptance: a general recognition that new revenues were needed to offset the $90 million General Fund deficit predicted for 1953; the fact that the BAT was originally proposed as an emergency tax, set to expire in 1955; the low statutory rate of one mill (.001 percent) on utilities and four mills (.004 percent) on all other business; inclusion of a farm lobby proposal for a specific dollar exemption of the first $10,000 of the adjusted receipts tax base; support from various business trade associations (farm, newspapers, manufacturing) at the time of enactment; the fact that the tax was written with the advice of industrial economists and attorneys — notably Ford and General Motors representatives; and the extensive and successful educational campaign conducted by the Revenue Division of the Department of Treasury. In the first few months following enactment of the statute, representatives of the Department of Treasury held seminars on the BAT in more than 200 meetings with service clubs, business and professional organizations, chambers of commerce, and eleemosynary groups in order to explain both the urgent need for increased state revenue and the theory and mechanics of the tax itself. As a result, department officials not only cleared up most of the questions regarding the new levy, but also enlisted the cooperation of many businessmen and newspapers in the education campaign.

Repeal

Despite predictions at the time of its enactment that the BAT would be unacceptable to the Michigan business community as well as to the courts, the tax received a widespread, positive reception from business, the judiciary, and most tax economists.[10] Nevertheless, the

---

9. See E. C. Stephenson, "The Michigan Business Activities Tax: A Retailer's Viewpoint," in *Proceedings of the Forty-Eighth Annual Conference on Taxation* (Columbus: National Tax Association, 1968), pp. 29–32; Donald K. Barnes, "The Anamalous Business Activities Tax," in *Proceedings of the Sixty-First Annual Conference on Taxation* (Columbus: National Tax Association, 1968), pp. 115–17; and Kent Sagendorf, "Truth about the New State Tax — It's Fair — Plays No Favorites," *Inside Michigan Magazine* 3 (May 1953): 18–19.

10. Legal critics questioned the constitutionality of the tax particularly with regard to the multistate allocation formula. See the remarks by Paul G. Kauper and Samuel D. Estep, "Interstate Transactions Covered by the Business Activities Tax," in *A Syllabus of the Presentation at the University of*

tax began to lose both political and professional support. According to Clarence W. Lock, Michigan Tax Commissioner at the time, the BAT ultimately was repealed not because of widespread dissatisfaction with the rationale or the actual economic and administrative characteristics of the tax, but because its proponents simply stopped vigorously defending it against periodic attempts to replace it with a corporate net income levy.[11] The result was that rather than eliminating, or at least minimizing, the defects of the BAT statute (for example, the minimum deduction provisions, or the inconsistency of treatment of capital purchases and depreciation), the legislature repealed the levy in the 1967 session and replaced it with a corporate and personal net income tax.[12]

Three identifiable schools of political and economic thought provided the issues regarding the BAT's suitability as the major form of business taxation in the Michigan fiscal system. They were: (1) those who argued that the BAT should be amended to eliminate its deviation from a value-added tax; (2) the no-profit, no-tax critics; and (3) the personal income taxation proponents. The strongest argument for the first group, and a defense of the value-added tax as a proper form of state business taxation, was made by James A. Papke in 1960.[13] Six years later, the Michigan State University tax study by Denzel Cline and Milton Taylor re-emphasized that the legislature could amend the BAT to a pure value-added levy rather than take the course of outright repeal.[14]

Michigan Law Institute (Ann Arbor: University of Michigan Press, 1953), pp. 11–20. For a complete discussion of the legal tests regarding the BAT see Peter A. Firmin, *The Michigan Business Receipts Tax* (Ann Arbor: University of Michigan Press, 1953).

11. Interview with Clarence W. Lock, Michigan Tax Commissioner, June 1969. This view is also presented by Denzel C. Cline and Milton C. Taylor, *Michigan Tax Reform* (East Lansing: Michigan State University Institute for Community Services, 1966), pp. 55–56. Several recommendations for a corporate net income replacement for the BAT are summarized by Paul W. McCracken in *Taxes and Economic Growth in Michigan*, edited by Paul W. McCracken (Kalamazoo: Upjohn Institute for Employment Research, 1960), pp. 10–12. One of the organized efforts to repeal the BAT was made by a Michigan citizens group in *A Program for Tax Reform*, A Report of the Subcommittee of Taxation of the Citizens for Michigan (Lansing: Citizens for Michigan, 1961).

12. Act 281, P.A. 1967.

13. James A. Papke, "Michigan's Value Added Tax after Seven Years," *National Tax Journal* 13 (December 1960): 350–63.

14. Cline and Taylor, *Tax Reform.*

From its inception one of the most widespread criticisms of the BAT was based on the no-profit, no-tax issue. Since the tax base consisted of property and payrolls in addition to net income, a business which made zero profits or even losses still would have a positive tax liability. This characteristic was inimical to the school of thought which supported either (or both) of the views that (1) the ability-to-pay doctrine provides the only logical rationale for taxing business, or (2) any tax which is not contingent upon business making a profit will impede industrial growth.[15]

Finally, there were those who saw the need for a personal income tax. Between 1958 and 1966 there were five major Michigan tax studies.[16] Although the various policy recommendations were not in complete agreement in advocating repeal of the BAT (indeed, a number of consultants argued that the BAT be retained as a minimum alternative on the zero profit firms), there was a consensus that a broad-based personal income tax would suffice as a tool to avoid chronic revenue–expenditure gaps.

---

15. This argument was also expressed in the terms that the BAT was a cost tax rather than a success tax. For a discussion of this issue see the articles by Harold Groves, E. M. Hoover, and Paul McCracken in *Taxes and Economic Growth*, pp. 87 ff, 131 ff, and 11.

16. The studies were: *Taxes and Economic Growth;* Cline and Taylor, *Tax Reform;* "Report of the Citizens Advisory Committee," in *Michigan Tax Study* (Lansing: 1958); *Michigan Tax Study Staff Papers* (Lansing: 1958), esp. chap. 20; and *The Michigan Economy: Prospects and Problems,* edited by Daniel R. Fusfeld (Kalamazoo: The Upjohn Institute for Employment Research, 1962), pp. 18–21.

Computation of the Tax Base

The Business Activities Tax was levied on the business taxpayer's adjusted receipts derived from or attributable to Michigan sources. The starting point for computing the tax base was the determination of gross receipts for tax purposes, that is, total business receipts less certain exclusions. Once this figure was obtained, the taxpayer (business enterprise) was given the option of taking a minimum standard deduction equal to 50 percent of gross receipts, or of itemizing certain allowable statutory deductions. Gross receipts for tax purposes, less total deductions, equaled the firm's adjusted receipts. In addition, the first $12,500 of taxable adjusted receipts were exempt from the tax.

Statutory Provisions

In brief, the mechanics of the tax computations were as follows:[1]

$$\begin{matrix} Total\ Gross \\ Business\ Receipts \end{matrix} - Exclusions = \begin{matrix} Gross\ Receipts\ for \\ Tax\ Purposes\ (GRTP) \end{matrix}[2]$$

---

1. The Business Activities Tax was imposed by Act 150, Public Laws of 1953, and was codified as Secs. 205.551 to 205.574 of the Compiled Laws of Michigan. A complete hypothetical sample of the tax computation is presented in Appendix A. Unless otherwise noted, footnote citations are based on laws as amended through 1967.

2. *Gross receipts,* for tax purposes, were defined as the entire amount re-

$$GRTP - \frac{50\% \text{ of } GRTP \text{ or}}{\text{Itemized Deductions}} = \text{Adjusted Receipts}$$

$$\frac{\text{Adjusted}}{\text{Receipts}} - \frac{\text{Specific Dollar}}{\text{Exemptions}} = \frac{\text{Taxable}}{\text{Base}}$$

Deductions

The BAT base was computed by subtracting from gross receipts all outlays, with certain exceptions, which were treated under the federal IRS code as ordinary and necessary expenses of conducting business.[3] These deductions included such items as cost of merchandise purchased (excluding labor or overhead costs), supplies, rent and interest paid, taxes (other than those on or measured by net income), utilities, and an allowance for the depreciation of real property.[4] The

---

ceived, or to be received, by any business activity (taxpayer) operating for gain or profit, on a cash or on a standard accounting accrual basis in money, credits, property, or other money's worth. Specifically excluded from the computation of the taxpayer's gross receipts were the following items: amounts received from the sale of capital assets which were not held for sale during the ordinary course of business; cash discounts and refunds allowed and taken; wages, salaries, or any compensation received for services rendered by an employee to his employer; amounts received as an agent on behalf of another; interest and dividends received; and, if the taxpayer's accounting was on an accrual basis, payments on accounts and notes receivable. Some items included in the definition of a taxpayer's gross receipts were: receipts from the sales of all property and/or services; commissions earned (except as an employee); income from professional services; rents and royalties received; and receipts from sales of scrap and other similar items except (as noted above) capital assets. Act 150, P. A. 1953, Sec. 205.551 and R. 205.560, Rule 10.

Historical notes: Prior to 1954, cash discounts and returned purchases were allowed as a deduction from adjusted receipts rather than as an exclusion as allowed after 1954. The net result of the original provision was to benefit taxpayers using the minimum standard deduction provision since they were, in effect, still allowed these deductions. Also prior to a 1961 amendment, royalty income was permitted as an exclusion from gross receipts.

3. Act 150, P. A. 1953, Sec. 205.551 and R. 205.561, Rule 11.

4. Ibid. *Real property* was defined to include all building, improvements, and fixtures which became a part of real estate (including appurtenances, improvements, and fixtures affixed to real property rented or leased by the taxpayer). Other examples of deductions were: advertising, insurance, losses from bad debts, freight, dues to business associations, business contributions to charitable organizations, fees for legal and professional services, rent paid for property used in business (including tool rental), travel expenses, repairs (other than those which are capitalized), payments to a trust when the trust is

deductability of these items was justified on the basis that they were interfirm purchases, that is, amounts paid which were included in the adjusted receipts of the selling enterprise and therefore taxed at an earlier stage of production. Consistent with this rationale, items such as wages, salaries, and all other compensations to employees, distributions to partners, dividends paid to stockholders, and an allowance for depreciation of the capitalization of payroll expenditures were not permitted as deductions since these items were not "paid to any business the income from which is subject to the tax."[5]

The statute also provided for two special deductions. First, if the total amount of the itemized deductions was less than 50 percent of the taxpayer's gross receipts, then the firm was permitted to take a standard deduction of a flat 50 percent of gross receipts. Second, a so-called excess payroll deduction further extended the amount of total allowable deductions to a maximum of 60 percent of gross receipts. If the firm's payroll exceeded 50 percent of gross receipts, a deduction of 10 percent of those receipts or one-half the excess of payroll over 50 percent, whichever was smaller, was permitted in addition to the minimum standard deduction. This provision applied only to taxpayers who used the flat 50 percent, rather than itemized, deductions.

To illustrate the mechanics of these special deductions, assume there are three representative firms as shown below. Firm A was eligible

	Firm A	Firm B	Firm C
Gross receipts	$50,000	$50,000	$50,000
Total itemized deductions	10,000	10,000	27,500
Payroll	20,000	38,000	20,000
Minimum deduction	25,000	25,000	Not applicable

exempt from federal income taxes under provisions of the IRS code, taxes withheld or collected from employees, taxes and fees other than on or measured by net income (for example, excise taxes from customers if included in the taxpayer's gross receipts, license fees, and local property taxes except those arising from special assessments on capital improvements), and depreciation on items of real estate which are carried on the taxpayer's accounting records as assets and which are subject to an allowance for depreciation or amortization for federal income tax purposes for the same taxable period.

5. Act 150, P. A. 1953, Sec. 205.561.

Additional payroll deduction	None	The smaller of 5,000 or 6,500	Not applicable
Total deduction as a percentage of gross receipts	50	60	55

for the minimum deduction, but could not also deduct the $10,000 of itemized expenses since that amount was included in the 50 percent. In addition, A did not qualify for the excess payroll deduction since the total payroll was less than 50 percent of its gross receipts. Firm B, on the other hand, was eligible for both special allowances, and, as a result, extended its total deduction to 60 percent of gross receipts — the maximum allowed under these special provisions. Finally, firm C, with total itemized deductions greater than 50 percent of gross receipts, would have elected to ignore the minimum standard deduction provision altogether. However, firm C was not eligible to consider the excess payroll deduction provision since it did not elect to use the minimum standard deduction.

Exemptions

Exemptions for certain types of business activity were provided for a variety of reasons.[6] These included: issues of constitutionality (for example, government agencies and instrumentalities); simplicity of compliance and administration (for example, casual or isolated transactions); and political expediency (private nonprofit organizations such as religious, charitable, scientific, literary, educational, and similar associations ostensibly performing public services). Financial institutions were specifically exempt on the grounds that they were subject to a special intangibles tax. Individuals receiving wages and salaries in an .employer–employee relationship were exempt because the tax was specifically levied on business enterprises.

In addition to organizational exemptions, the Michigan statute also granted a specific dollar exemption of the first $12,500 of adjusted receipts to all taxpayers. The effect of this exemption, in conjunction with the minimum standard deduction, was to exclude from the tax all businesses not having over $25,000 in gross receipts; businesses

---

6. Act 150, P. A. 1953, R. 205.563, Rule 13; and Sec. 205.554.

with smaller receipts were not required to file a return. Only one such specific dollar exemption was granted per taxpayer, even though he may have engaged in more than one business activity. For example, a corporation or a partnership (of any size or number of partners) was considered a separate taxable entity and therefore was entitled to a single $12,500 exemption. If the business operated for less than one year, the exemption was prorated for the period of activity.

Other Provisions

MULTISTATE INCOME. The BAT was levied on the adjusted receipts derived from or attributable to Michigan sources.[7] In order to apportion receipts attributable to Michigan, taxpayers deriving receipts both from within and without Michigan had the option of using separate accounting methods acceptable to the tax commissioner, or a statutory allocation formula provided by the BAT. In the original statute the taxable receipts of a firm were those from Michigan sales exclusively plus 50 percent of receipts from interstate transactions. This formula used only sales as a measure of economic activity and, in addition, the 50 percent figure was arbitrarily written into the statute.[8]

In the 1955 legislative session the one-factor formula was replaced with a three-factor (payroll, property, and sales by destination) formula. Until the repeal of the act in 1967, a firm allocated its adjusted receipts to Michigan by computing the simple average of the ratio of Michigan property to total property, Michigan payroll to total payroll, and Michigan receipts to total receipts. The statute also provided special apportionment formulas for various transportation services. Receipts derived from pipeline transportation were allocated by barrel miles (oil) or cubic feet miles (gas); other carriers' receipts attributable to Michigan were allocated on the ratio of a firm's revenue miles in Michigan to revenue miles everywhere.

NET INCOME CREDIT. Once the taxpaying firm had arrived at its taxable adjusted receipts (gross receipts less total deduction and specific

---

7. Act 150, P. A. 1953, Sec. 205.553 and R. 205.556, Rule 16.

8. According to one Michigan observer, the 50 percent figure was arrived at because "generally speaking, it was estimated that materials and supplies purchased by manufacturing industries will average between 45 percent and 55 percent and, therefore, 50 percent was picked as a figure which would equalize the service and professional taxpayers with industry generally." See Alan Gornick, *The Michigan Business Receipts Tax*, pp. 13–14.

dollar exemption) and computed the tax due, it was entitled to a variable tax credit based on the ratio of 1 percent of the firm's adjusted receipts to net income.[9] The resulting percentage for credit purposes was not to be less than 1 percent or greater than 25 percent. Negative credits were not allowed.[10]

TAX RATE. The BAT incorporated a dual-rate scheme.[11] Public utilities originally were taxed at 1 mill per dollar of adjusted receipts, and all other business was taxed at a 4-mill rate. At the beginning of fiscal 1955 the rates were increased to 1½ and 6½ mills respectively. The rates were increased for the last time in 1959, to 2 mills for utilities and 7¾ mills for all other business.

Administrative Procedures

Only those businesses having annual gross receipts of more than $25,000 were required to file a return, and the taxpayer could pay either in quarterly installments, or, with approval from the Department of Treasury, in advance for the entire year, on a cash receipts or accrual basis.[12] The first three quarterly returns required the business to make estimates of only four items: gross receipts, total deductions, taxable balance (gross receipts less deductions), and tax due. At the end of the taxpayer's fiscal year the firm filled out an annual return.

---

9. Act 150, P. A. 1953, Sec. 205.552 as amended. This provision was added to the BAT statute in 1959.

10. To illustrate the mechanics of the credit, assume a firm had adjusted receipts of $30,000 and a net income of $1,500. The tax due was then reduced by 20 percent $\dfrac{1 \text{ percent of Adjusted Receipts}}{\text{Net Income}}$. Given a 7¾ mill tax rate, the tax due would be reduced from $232.50 to $186.00.

Certain expenses such as payroll, depreciation allowances for personal property, and city or state income taxes were not deductible in computing the adjusted receipts tax base; they were allowed as deductions in arriving at net income. See Act 262, Laws 1959 as amended to Act 150, P. A. 1953, Sec. 205.551.

11. Act 150, P. A. 1953, Sec. 205.552.

12. Ibid. Sec. 205.555, 205.560, and R. 205.551, Rule 1.

4

Economic Nature of the
Business Activities Tax

The Michigan statute was commonly designated by state officials as a specific tax on business income. A general business tax, it was levied on corporate and unincorporated businesses, extending from the agricultural and extractive industries to the service trades and the professions. Theoretically, the size of the tax base could be computed using either the legally required subtraction approach (gross business receipts less certain specified expenses incurred in the conduct of normal business operations), or the addition method (sum of the firm's profit and payroll and personal property depreciation expenses).

Administrators, legal experts, and students of public finance alike were unable to agree on a precise classification of the tax. The Commerce Clearing House described the levy as "basically a gross receipts tax and in some respects a net income and sales tax." The Bureau of the Census of the United States Department of Commerce classified it under "other taxes" rather than include it in a sales, income, or gross receipts category, and the Advisory Commission on Intergovernmental Relations placed the BAT in a "gross receipts — general sales tax" category.[1] However, since the BAT was a levy on

---

1. Commerce Clearing House, *Michigan Tax Reports* (Chicago: Commerce

the business enterprise at the point of origin of income and product, and was applied to the difference between what a firm receives in sales proceeds and what it spends in purchasing goods and services from other firms, it was classified by most economists as a value-added type levy.[2] The Michigan Department of Treasury insisted that the BAT was a broad-based income tax. However, in order to avoid confusing it with either the conventional net profits or gross receipts levies, the department used the designation "Business Activities Tax."

The question of classification had important administrative and legal implications well beyond the conceptual economic issue. The Michigan Supreme Court accepted the Department of Treasury's interpretation and held that although the BAT was substantially broader than a tax on net income, it was, nevertheless, *an income tax*.[3] Once the tax was thus classified, other court decisions, especially those upholding the right of a state to tax interstate business, applied to the Michigan statute. Had the courts not so ruled, the legal income tax precedents permitting the taxation of multistate receipts would not have applied to the BAT and, as a result, the revenue productivity features of the tax would have been greatly restricted.[4]

Conceptual Classification

The economic nature of a tax is defined by whether it is broad or narrow based, direct or indirect, and is on fixed or variable costs. The

---

Clearing House, Inc., 1967), Para. 65-003; U.S. Department of Commerce, Bureau of the Census, *State Tax Collections* (Washington, D.C.: U.S. Government Printing Office, 1967), Table 9; and Advisory Commission on Intergovernmental Relations, *State and Local Finance: Significant Features 1966–1969*, Report M-43 (Washington, D.C.: U.S. Government Printing Office, 1968).

2. See, for example, the interpretations by Clarence W. Lock, Donovan J. Rau, and Howard D. Hamilton, "The Michigan Value Added Tax," *National Tax Journal* 7 (December 1955): 357–71; Francisco Forte, "On the Feasibility of a Truly General Value Added Tax: Some Reflections on the French Experience," *National Tax Journal* 12 (December 1966): 337–61; Richard Malt, "Some Aspects of a Value Added Tax for Canada," in *Queens University Papers in Taxation and Public Finance*, edited by J. R. Allan and I. J. Goffman (Kingston: Queens University, Canadian Tax Foundation, 1966), pp. 52–53; and Lindholm, "Value Added Tax: Review."

3. *Armco Steel Corporation* v. *State of Michigan, et al.* (1960), 102 N.W. For a discussion of the legal issues involved, see Donald K. Barnes, "The Business Receipts Tax," *Michigan State Bar Journal* 33 (October 1953): 31–39.

4. A summary of the litigation is given in *Michigan Tax Reports*, para. 65-217 to 65-218, pp. 659–61, and Firmin, *Business Receipts Tax*.

BAT can be described as a broad (general) tax since it was levied on business activity common to all types and legal forms of business rather than on production process inputs or final commodities that were specific to only certain taxpayer groups.

A direct tax traditionally is one removed from subsequent market transactions, for example, a payroll or personal income tax. Indirect taxes are more closely associated with further market transactions. Examples would be sales, excise, or production levies which, presumably, are shifted from the taxpayer to some other economic unit.[5] Because the BAT was levied on business — an intermediary or conduit in the economic process — and was based on a measure of production, it is included in the indirect tax classification.

Finally, the BAT can be considered in the variable rather than fixed cost category. The tax was based on the value of real property, labor, and entrepreneurial resources used, and, as a result, varied with changes in total cost directly corresponding to these input–final output relationships. That is, the BAT was an addition to average variable and marginal costs of the firm rather than a lump sum charge on the firm's operations.

A Comparison

To gain a better understanding of the economic nature of the BAT statute, it will be useful to make some comparisons between the tax and gross receipts, net income, and value-added levies. Various general computational procedures are presented in Table 2.

Gross Receipts and Net Income

Similar to a gross receipts tax, the BAT was assessed regardless of the level of profitability or loss, and did not permit a deduction for payrolls. However, the similarity ends there. While the gross receipts taxes enacted by some states permit a limited number of deductions, the deductions from gross receipts allowed by the Business Activities Tax were different in nature and were based on a markedly different philosophy.[6] In particular, the deductions from a pure gross receipts

---

5. John F. Due, *Government Finance: Economics of the Public Sector,* 4th ed. (Homewood, Ill.: Richard D. Irwin, Inc., 1968), p. 87 ff. As Due points out, this direct–indirect classification has little practical value.

6. Firmin, *Business Receipts Tax,* p. 9.

levy are based on the reasoning that the permitted deduction is, in essence, not part of actual business receipts, whereas the deductions in the BAT statute were justified as the interfirm purchases of materials, supplies, and the like. As a result, the BAT was much more a net levy than are gross receipts or turnover taxes. The BAT base was substantially broader than the base of a conventional business net income or profits levy. It included, in addition to profits before taxes, the firm's payrolls, depreciation of fixed assets other than estate, and depletion costs.

Value Added

The BAT was a broad-based levy on income generated at the source of production. It essentially approximated the economist's concept of a value-added tax — the sum of net dollar value contributed by the business enterprise to the output of goods and services of the state. In order to examine the question of how closely the Michigan tax conformed to a pure value-added tax, it is useful to review the three categories of value-added taxes — the net income, consumption, and gross product bases[7] — and explicitly to compare them to the computational approach to the BAT. Because the classifications of the various types of value-added taxes hinge on the treatment of specific items, reference should be made to the entries presented in Table 2, columns 4-6.

CAPITAL ON FORCE ACCOUNT. If a firm produces its own plant and equipment (investment on force account), there has been an addition to the economy's output. Both net income and gross product bases of value-added taxation recognize this activity as an addition to output, and the value (usually as measured by the firm's direct cost outlay, since there is no final market valuation) is not deducted from the tax base. However, unlike the income variant, which permits deduction for capital depreciation in subsequent years, the gross product variant permits no such write-off. In computing the consumption variant of the value-added tax, the firm neither adds the value of in-

---

7. Carl S. Shoup, "Theory and Background of the Value Added Tax," in *Proceedings of the Forty-Eighth Annual Conference on Taxation* (Columbus: National Tax Association, 1955), pp. 7–19; and Clara K. Sullivan, *The Tax on Value Added* (New York: Columbia University Press, 1965), pp. 179–213. These various classifications of the value tax were first discussed in the Shoup article.

vestment on force account to its tax base, nor does it deduct depreciation on that capital. In essence, the firm has sold the capital equipment to itself and subtracted it as it would any other business purchase.[8]

The treatment of investment on force account items in the BAT was a hybrid of the foregoing approaches. Although the total cost of providing investment on force account was not added and, therefore, was not specifically included in the individual firm's tax base, that part of the cost of investment which could be identified as payroll expenditure was included due to the explicit ruling that no element of payroll expenditures of a firm to its own labor qualified as a statutory deduction.[9] Furthermore, a depreciation deduction for such force account investment was allowed in subsequent years only if the investment happened to qualify as real property. Thus, the BAT would be more net than the gross product variant, but broader than either the consumption or income variant of a value-added tax.

NET INVENTORY CHANGE. Similar to the income and gross product value-added bases and the conventional net profits approach, the BAT included any net inventory accumulation as an addition to the tax base. Conversely, a net reduction in annual inventory stock was subtracted from the tax base. This procedure was justified on the grounds that even if a business firm had final sales receipts equal to interfirm purchases, but used its productive factors during the year to produce goods which went into year-end inventories, this production should be viewed as the firm's value added, that is, the firm's contribution to social output. However, if in a subsequent accounting period the firm did nothing but sell those inventories, its contribution to social output (value added) would equal the excess of the final sales price over the book value of the products in inventory. In particular, the BAT accounted for this inventory change by specifically defining the cost-of-goods-sold deduction as beginning inventory plus merchandise purchased for resale or manufacturing less ending inventory.

In contrast to the BAT approach, the consumption variant for computing value added permits a deduction for inventory accumulation, in effect treating it as a capital outlay and allowing immediate expensing. Inventory reductions in a subsequent year are included in the net sales component of the value-added base. Again the basic dif-

8. Shoup, "Theory and Background," p. 14.
9. Act 150, P. A. 1953, R. 205.561, Rule 11.

TABLE 2. Computation of Various Business Tax Bases

1 BAT base	2 Gross receipts base	3 Net income base	4 Value added: consumption base	5 Value added: income base	6 Value added: gross product base
Net receipts from sales, services, rent, and interest	Gross receipts from sales of goods and/or services	Net receipts from sales, services, rent, and interest	Net receipts from sales, services, rent, and interest	Net receipts from sales, services, rent, and interest	Net receipts from sales, services, rent, and interest
PLUS Investment on force account		PLUS Investment on force account		PLUS Investment on force account	PLUS Investment on force account
PLUS Net inventory accumulation		PLUS Net inventory accumulation		PLUS Net inventory accumulation	PLUS Net inventory accumulation
PLUS Owner's personal consumption of firm's products		PLUS Owner's personal consumption of firm's products	PLUS Owner's personal consumption of firm's products	PLUS Owner's personal consumption of firm's products	PLUS Owner's personal consumption of firm's products

MINUS	MINUS	MINUS	MINUS	MINUS	MINUS
Current account purchases of goods and services from other business (including rent and interest paid)	Some statutes allow deductions for returned sales, cash discounts, installation and transportation charges incurred on sale and/or delivery of merchandise, and taxes not directly measured by income (such as excise taxes)	Ordinary and necessary expenses incurred in the production of income (including payroll, interest paid, rent paid, and depreciation and depletion)	All purchases from other business (including capital asset purchases, interest, and rent paid)	Current account purchases of goods and services from other business (including rent and interest paid)	Current account purchases of goods and services from other business (including rent and interest paid)
MINUS Depreciation on real property				**MINUS** Depreciation on real and personal property	

Sources: Clara K. Sullivan, *The Tax on Value Added* (New York: Columbia University Press, 1965), chap. 5; and Commerce Clearing House, Inc., *Michigan Tax Reports: Business Activities Tax* (Chicago: Commerce Clearing House, 1967), pp. 6551-669.

ference between the consumption and income, or BAT, approach is one of timing.

CAPITAL EXPENDITURES. A most important issue in computing the value-added or adjusted receipts tax base is the treatment given capital expenditures. Indeed, the major difference in the four approaches (consumption, income, gross product, and adjusted receipts bases) revolves around this issue. As was true with the treatment of capital investment on force account, the consumption base employs the simplest administrative treatment for all capital expenditures. In particular, the consumption variant permits immediate expensing of capital assets (instantaneous depreciation), and then disallows any deduction for future depreciation or amortization.[10] The income variant does not permit the immediate deduction of capital asset purchases, but permits depreciation and amortization allowances on both real and personal property in subsequent years. Thus, both the consumption and income variants for computing value added are net of capital outlays, with the time period for the expensing becoming the operational issue.

The gross product value-added base ignores the issue of capital asset purchases altogether by disallowing immediate expensing of both capital asset purchases and depreciation allowances. In fact, it is this complete inclusion of capital in the tax base which gives the gross product variant its label. As originally enacted, the Michigan adjusted receipts base conformed to the gross-value-added concept. However, after the 1955 amendments the BAT became a combination of the gross product and the net income base types.[11]

Quantitative Comparison

Considering the general computational nature of the adjusted receipts base, the BAT was more similar to the income variant than to either of the other value-added approaches. Accordingly, in order to make comparisons of the major components of the BAT with a value-added levy, the net income variant of the value-added base was used. Table 3 presents the variations, by major industry type, of the com-

---

10. Carl Shoup discusses a second capital exemption value-added base, the wages type tax. See Carl S. Shoup, *Public Finance* (Chicago: Aldine Press, 1969), pp. 252–53.

11. Act 282, Laws 1955. This act provided a deduction for depreciation or amortization of real property.

ponents of the Michigan income variant value-added tax base. The measure employed the addition computational approach, and was based on the principle that the value added of a business operation is equivalent to the individual firm's contribution to net national income which it pays out in payroll, interest and rents, and the profit it earns. In essence, it is a figure which directly measures the extent of the productive activities of the employees of the firm, the services rendered by individual creditors and lessors of the firm, and the reward to entrepreneurs for bearing risk and skills in organization.[12]

TABLE 3. Michigan Value-Added Tax Base Components,
by Industry, 1965

| Industry | Percentage of tax base | | | | |
	Payroll	*Rents*	*Interest*	*Profit*[a]	*Total*
Agriculture	56.2	8.5	8.3	26.8	100.0
Mining	59.3	2.0	3.5	35.0	100.0
Construction	86.3	1.8	1.8	9.9	100.0
Manufacturing	69.8	2.4	2.1	25.4	100.0
Utilities	57.6	5.2	8.2	28.8	100.0
Wholesale trade	63.7	6.1	4.5	25.5	100.0
Retail trade	61.4	15.0	3.6	19.7	100.0
Services	75.3	8.0	3.9	12.7	100.0
All industry[b]	69.7	4.6	3.4	22.1	100.0

SOURCES: Computed from tax returns (1965) supplied by Michigan Department of Treasury, Revenue Division; U.S. Department of Treasury, Internal Revenue Service, *Statistics of Income: Business Income Tax Returns* and *Corporation Income Tax Returns* (Washington, D.C.: Government Printing Office, 1965), Tables 2, 3, and 5; and Daniel B. Suits, *Econometric Model of Michigan*, Technical Report No. 3 (Lansing: Michigan Department of Commerce, 1966), pp. 15–19 and Appendix A.
NOTE: Details may not add to totals due to rounding.
[a]Includes estimate for income taxes.
[b]Weighted average.

---

12. The treatment of rent creates a problem in computing business value added. Under the pure value-added concept rent is considered a payment for supply of business services. Therefore, the individual firm's employment of these services is measured by the amount of rent paid and becomes a component of its value added. Nevertheless, this interpretation was not accepted in the BAT computation. Rather, the individual or business which offered the land/property service was considered as the entity adding value to society's net product, and therefore rent received, not paid, was considered as part of the tax base. In completely closed (circular plan) economy framework, the aggregate value-added base is the same for both approaches. In the subnational economy, however, the base is larger (smaller) if the taxing jurisdiction is a net rent receiver (payer).

Table 4 presents the percentage distribution, by industry, of the components which comprise the Michigan BAT base. Unlike the computation of the value-added figure, the Michigan adjusted receipts tax base is computed by summing payrolls (not including amounts paid to proprietors or partners), personal property depreciation, state and city income taxes, and business net income.

TABLE 4.   Percentage of BAT Adjusted Receipts
Components, by Industry, 1965

| Industry | Percentage of tax base components | | | | |
	Payroll	Depreciation	Profits	Taxes	Total
Agriculture	54.5	12.6	26.0	6.7	100.0
Mining	50.2	8.5	29.7	11.4	100.0
Construction	82.7	4.9	9.5	2.7	100.0
Manufacturing	72.3	4.8	22.7	10.0	100.0
Utilities	50.7	12.4	25.3	11.3	100.0
Wholesale trade	62.0	4.3	24.8	8.7	100.0
Retail trade	64.9	6.9	20.9	7.2	100.0
Services	72.6	11.3	12.2	3.7	100.0
All industry[a]	62.4	6.5	21.8	9.1	100.0

SOURCES: Computed from tax return data (1965) supplied by Michigan Department of Treasury, Revenue Division; U.S. Department of Treasury, Internal Revenue Service, *Statistics of Income: Business Tax Returns* (Washington, D.C.: Government Printing Office, 1965); and Daniel B. Suits, *Econometric Model of Michigan,* Technical Report No. 3 (Lansing: Michigan Department of Commerce, 1966), pp. 15–19 and Appendix A.

NOTE: Details may not add to totals due to rounding.

[a]Weighted average.

It is apparent from a comparison of Tables 3 and 4 that for both the value-added tax and the Business Activities Tax payrolls and profits are quantitatively the most important tax base components. In all the industry illustrations, the percentage figures of payroll to total tax base and profit to total tax base are comparable. That both the taxes considered here are largely based on payrolls and profits is further indicated by the fact that the rent-plus-interest share of the value-added levy accounts for approximately 10 percent of the total tax base, and the depreciation-plus-taxes share of adjusted receipts is just over 15 percent of the total base. The fact that percentages of the tax base components are nearly the same for the value-added and adjusted receipts computations supports the view that, empirically, the *de facto* composition of the BAT base closely approximated the composition of an income type value-added levy.

A Value-Added Tax?

Although in principle the BAT was a value-added tax (net income variant), there were significant deviations from the pure value-added tax concept.

> As is always true in the formulation of tax policy legislative discretion was employed to temper the rigidities of formal theory. Although departures from the theory of value-added taxation were in some applications necessary, as being consistent with accepted practices in state taxation, others, however, especially the major ones, lack rationale and tend to negate the merits of the form of taxation.[13]

It is extremely important to emphasize that a truly general tax base can rarely, if ever, be achieved once existing institutional constraints, legal and political as well as economic, are introduced into the tax policy-making process. This is true despite the fact that a comprehensive tax base can be analytically defined.

> [Although] . . . the concept of a comprehensive tax base is subject to [an] analytically precise definition . . . the definition cannot be applied consistently in practice, but it is a useful *ad hoc* instrument for provoking the right questions, not for supplying the right answers. . . . Tax experts, whether lawyers or economists, should recognize that legal and economic considerations are so interwoven in the issues of tax policy that recommendations which ignore realistic institutional constraints, either legal or economic in nature, are likely to be constructive only by chance or if confined to narrowly technical matters.[14]

For economic purposes it is as reasonable to classify the BAT as a

---

13. Papke, "Michigan's Value Added Tax," pp. 356–57.

14. Henry Aaron, "What Is a Comprehensive Tax Base Anyway?" *National Tax Journal* 22 (December 1969): 543–49. The issue of the near impossibility of designing a truly general value-added tax which falls impartially on all consumption or income was also examined in the article by Forte, "Feasibility of a Truly General Value Added Tax." However, in 1967 and again in 1968 the West Virginia legislature considered a statute which conceptually was very close to a pure value-added tax, but was written, for litigation purposes, as an income tax. The 1968 measure was approved by the legislature but vetoed by the governor. For a discussion see Robert D. Ebel and James A. Papke, "A Closer Look at the Value Added Tax: Propositions and Implications," in *Proceedings of the Sixtieth Annual Conference on Taxation* (Columbus: National Tax Association, 1967), pp. 161–69; and Dennis R. Leyden, "Some Empirical Observations on the Differential Impact of a Turnover Versus Value Added Tax at the Subnational Level," unpublished manuscript draft for the Bureau of Business Research, West Virginia University, 1971, p. 14 ff.

form of value-added tax as it is to call the federal tax on corporate income a net income levy.[15]

A Retail Sales Tax?

One of the conventional criticisms of a value-added tax such as the BAT is that it is, in effect, no more than a retail sales tax. This criticism deserves further attention, especially since the argument can have important implications for policy makers.

The Closed Economy

The main focus of the academic discussion regarding the nature of value-added taxation has been almost entirely concentrated within a national, or even supernational, framework.[16] Indeed, when the tax

---

15. Conventional corporate net income taxes deviate from the analytically comprehensive concept of taxable business net income. The statutory provisions for exemptions of various financial institutions, the definition of corporations, measures of depreciation and depletion, deductibility of interest, some types of inventory treatment, receipts of cooperatives, income from foreign sources, and the treatment of intercorporate dividends are examples of the divergence between the practical and theoretical views of the scope of taxable net income.

16. For example, see the following: *The Role of Direct and Indirect Taxes in the Federal Revenue System,* a Conference Report of the National Bureau of Economic Research and the Brookings Institution, Studies of Government Finance, The Brookings Institution (Princeton: Princeton University Press, 1964); Forte, "On the Feasibility of a Truly General Value Added Tax"; L. G. Sandberg, "A Value Added Tax for Sweden," *National Tax Journal* 17 (September 1964): 292–96; Sullivan, *Tax on Value Added;* John F. Due, "Proposals for a Federal Value Added Tax," *Illinois Business Review* (Spring 1970), p. 6 ff.; Richard Malt, "Value Added Tax for Canada," *Business Taxation,* A Report of the President's Task Force on Business Taxation (Washington, D.C.: U.S. Government Printing Office, 1970), pp. 61–75; Committee for Economic Development Research and Policy Committee, *Better Balance in Federal Taxes on Business* (New York: Committee for Economic Development, 1966), p. 37; Carl S. Shoup, ed., *Fiscal Harmonization in Common Markets* (New York: Columbia University Press, 1966); Maurice D. Weinrobe, "Corporate Taxes and United States Balance of Trade," *National Tax Journal* 24 (March 1971): 79–86; and B. Kenneth Sanden, "Value Added Tax: Application and Practice," in *Proceedings of the Sixty-Fourth Annual Conference on Taxation* (Columbus: National Tax Association, forthcoming). Two recent VAT bibliographies are Lindholm, "Value Added Tax: Review," pp. 1185–89; and Tax Foundation, *Research Bibliography: Value Added Taxes* (New York: the Foundation, 1971).

is considered within a national context, it is, in an accounting sense, a form of federal retail sales taxation.

As is a value-added tax, the general retail sales tax is levied on all consumer purchases of goods and services. Furthermore, if one adopts the consumption approach (Table 2, column 4) of computing value added, the total size of the base is, in fact, equivalent to the consumer's spending on all goods and services currently produced. Since this consumption variant of value added is calculated entirely on a current account basis, the tax base is the sum of the margins between gross sales and intermediate business purchases at each of the various stages of production, from manufacturing to wholesale and retail distribution. By definition this sum is equivalent to the final retail prices of consumer goods and services. Accordingly, it follows that an equal tax rate applied to the consumption value-added base and retail sales prices of currently rendered consumer services or goods would provide equal revenue yields for any one accounting period.[17]

An extension of this reasoning indicates that the gross product type of the value-added tax (Table 2, column 6) is also equivalent to a retail sales tax provided that the retail sales base is defined to include producers' capital as well as consumers' goods and services. In this case the value-added tax base is definitionally equal to gross domestic product, which is computed by subtracting all intermediate current account purchases from total sales receipts.

Unlike the consumption and gross product approaches to the computation of value added, the net income variant (Table 2, column 5) has no retail sales tax equivalent. The income type explicitly differentiates between business purchases on capital and current account bases by permitting a statutory deduction for depreciation of all investment goods. As a result, the net income type, when summed over the entire closed economy, is equivalent to society's net national income.

---

17. This assumes that once the value-added tax is introduced subsequent deductions for the existing capital stock (either instantaneous depreciation of the remaining life of the asset or continued schedular depreciation) are disallowed. This issue of the conditions for which value-added taxes and their equivalent tax bases have the same economic (relative price) effects is reviewed and discussed by Ann F. Friedlaender, "Incidence and Price Effects of Value Added Taxes," in *Proceedings of the Sixty-Fourth Annual Conference on Taxation* (Columbus: National Tax Association, forthcoming).

The Open Economy

The issue of the economic nature of various forms of the value-added tax changes once one moves tax policy considerations from a closed to an open tax jurisdiction context. This, of course, is particularly relevant to the Michigan Business Activities Tax experience. Specifically, unlike the closed economy, the open tax jurisdiction cannot restrict the flow of goods and services at any stage by erecting economic barriers such as tariffs, quotas, or import licenses. Similarly, open jurisdictions cannot artifically control the interstate movement of such factors of production as labor, capital, and entrepreneurial skills. Consequently, a high degree of mobility for final products and/or factors of production changes the economic character of subnational tax policy from that of structurally similar national policies.

There are two important implications of this economic openness for tax policy. First, just as subnational taxing jurisdictions cannot directly tax nonresidents (businesses and/or individuals) for using the services of that jurisdiction, resident individuals and/or businesses can engage in spending beyond the jurisdictional authority of their government. Second, goods and services produced within a state can be exported to residents of other taxing jurisdictions. Thus a tax such as the BAT which includes within its scope all product originating within a tax jurisdiction will be paid in part by nonresident factor owners, consumers, and wealth holders. This is quite unlike a retail sales tax, which is confined to final sales stages and, with minor exceptions such as tourists or traveling businessmen, is wholly paid by the residents of the taxing jurisdiction.

5

Business Activities Tax
Collections

A major characteristic of the BAT was its actual and potential revenue productivity. The BAT was proposed originally as a measure which was capable of eliminating a chronic revenue–expenditure gap in the Michigan General Fund. Most tax analysts, critics as well as proponents of the form of the BAT, agreed that the tax did have the ability to provide needed government revenues.[1]

Current Year Collections
Following the initial statutory amendments, the BAT was consistently the second largest source of state General Fund revenues, exceeded only by the retail sales tax; after 1958 the BAT was the third largest revenue producer in the entire fiscal structure.[2] During the life of the tax it increased in relation to total collections more than

---

1. For example, see papers presented in the sessions on the BAT in the 1955 and 1968 *Proceedings of the Annual Conference on Taxation* of the National Tax Association.
2. Michigan Department of Treasury, *Annual Report,* 1953–1967. All motor fuel tax revenue, except license fees, is earmarked for the Motor Vehicle Fund, the Waterways Fund, or the Aeronautics Fund.

any of the other Michigan tax levies. Whereas all state taxes except for the use tax and the BAT contributed a smaller share to total revenues in 1967 than in 1954, the BAT more than doubled its percentage share over this thirteen-year period.

Tables 5 and 6 present revenue data for various years and reflect discretionary legislative changes in both the rates and the bases (for example, changes in exemptions, allocation formulas, deductions).

TABLE 5.   Collections by Type of Tax, in Thousands
of Dollars, 1954–1967

Year	Retail sales tax[a]	Motor fuel tax[a]	BAT	Cigarette tax	Use tax
1954	275,420	88,913	23,423	25,981	13,825
1955	286,232	94,060	29,976	25,513	15,654
1956	308,683	132,990	59,448	26,745	18,481
1957	309,206	135,845	64,316	27,233	20,261
1958	298,347	136,579	60,727	43,370	19,691
1959	301,425	138,611	55,326	46,541	19,740
1960	323,582	146,331	72,305	53,812	40,145
1961	354,060	148,307	72,797	63,677	36,817
1962	427,174	152,639	68,274	51,486	34,188
1963	455,558	158,313	77,882	68,564	45,155
1964	487,405	167,251	89,938	70,341	50,889
1965	537,189	178,040	99,888	74,022	57,573
1966	589,669	190,501	119,221	76,648	68,640
1967	609,644	197,468	128,217	78,001	71,643

SOURCE: Michigan Department of Treasury, Revenue Division, *Annual Report* (Lansing: the Department, 1953–1968).
[a]All or part of tax was earmarked for non-General Fund disposition.
[b]Biannual collections for 1957.
[c]Inheritance, chain store, and severance taxes.

TABLE 5 — *Continued*

Year	Intangibles tax[a]	Utility property tax[b]	Corporation fee (ACPF)	Other[c]	Total
1954	17,230	15,053	44,520	11,860	516,225
1955	18,786	15,951	51,030	11,642	548,844
1956	21,338	17,765	56,370	9,701	651,521
1957	23,691	9,716	58,840	12,125	673,358
1958	24,245	20,841	64,070	11,675	679,545
1959	24,618	22,352	65,700	15,485	689,789
1960	27,103	23,702	68,490	13,436	768,906
1961	29,891	25,035	70,950	16,155	817,689
1962	31,731	25,166	75,410	16,243	882,331
1963	33,828	25,728	75,950	18,554	959,532
1964	34,604	26,850	82,550	16,618	1,026,446
1965	37,269	28,294	87,861	19,336	1,119,472
1966	44,292	30,701	92,766	24,359	1,236,797
1967	46,951	33,203	109,526	22,370	1,297,023

Table 7 examines the BAT's relationship *vis-à-vis* the other types of Michigan taxes, using information that explicitly takes into account legislative changes for all these specific levies. In particular, Table 7 presents adjusted data for a twelve-year period of Department of Treasury tax collections in Michigan, consistent with 1965 rates and bases.[3] Using this adjusted data, Table 8 was constructed in order to

TABLE 6. Percentage Distribution of Collections, by Type of Tax, 1954–1967

Year	Retail sales tax	Motor fuel tax	BAT	Cigarette tax	Use tax
1954	53.4	17.2	4.5	5.0	2.7
1955	52.1	17.1	5.5	4.6	2.9
1956	47.4	20.4	9.1	4.1	2.8
1957	45.9	20.2	9.6	4.0	3.0
1958	43.9	20.1	8.9	6.4	2.9
1959	43.7	20.1	8.1	6.7	2.9
1960	42.1	19.0	9.4	7.0	5.2
1961	43.3	18.1	8.9	7.8	4.5
1962	48.4	17.3	7.8	5.8	3.9
1963	47.5	16.5	8.1	7.1	4.7
1964	47.5	16.3	8.8	6.9	5.0
1965	48.0	15.9	8.9	6.6	5.1
1966	47.6	15.4	9.6	6.2	5.5
1967	47.0	15.2	9.9	6.0	5.5

SOURCE: Table 5.
NOTE: Details may not add to totals due to rounding.

TABLE 6 — Continued

Year	Intangibles tax	Utility property tax	Corporation fee (ACPF)	Other	Total
1954	3.3	2.9	8.6	2.3	100.0
1955	3.4	2.8	9.3	2.1	100.0
1956	3.3	2.7	8.7	1.5	100.0
1957	3.5	1.4	8.7	1.8	100.0
1958	3.6	3.1	9.4	1.7	100.0
1959	3.6	3.2	9.5	2.2	100.0
1960	3.5	3.1	8.9	1.7	100.0
1961	3.7	3.1	8.7	1.9	100.0
1962	3.6	2.9	8.5	1.8	100.0
1963	3.5	2.7	7.9	1.9	100.0
1964	3.3	2.6	8.0	1.6	100.0
1965	3.3	2.5	7.8	1.7	100.0
1966	3.6	2.5	7.5	2.0	100.0
1967	3.6	2.6	8.4	1.7	100.0

---

3. No adjustments were made prior to 1956 because of changes in the formula for interstate apportionment of the BAT base during these years.

examine the relative importance of the BAT *vis-à-vis* the other major taxes collected by the state.

As is indicated by the index number in Table 8, the BAT and the use tax show the largest relative growth in collections. From 1960–1967, the BAT grew 77 percent; the other two major revenue sources, the retail sales tax and the Annual Corporate Franchise Fee (ACPF),

TABLE 7. Collections, in Thousands of Dollars, Consistent
with 1965 Rates and Bases, 1956–1967

Year	Retail sales tax	Motor fuel tax	BAT	Cigarette tax
1956	410,728	132,845[a]	63,790	62,291
1957	411,391	135,845	69,129	63,433
1958	396,870	136,579	65,219	62,280
1959	401,014	138,611	59,276[a]	65,062
1960	430,550	146,331	72,305	68,250
1961	416,990[a]	148,307	72,797	69,122
1962	426,320	152,630	68,274	71,816
1963	454,720	158,313	77,882	70,500[a]
1964	486,640	167,251	89,938	70,260
1965	536,389	178,040	99,888	73,971
1966	589,422	190,051	119,221	76,645
1967	609,659	197,468	128,217	78,010

SOURCES: Harvey E. Brazer et al., *General Fund Estimates of Revenue and Expenditures to 1975*, Technical Report No. 11 (Lansing: Michigan Department of Commerce, 1967); Michigan Department of Treasury, Revenue Division, *Annual Report* (Lansing: the Department, 1953–1968); and *Executive Budget*, State of Michigan (Lansing: Office of the Governor, selected years).
[a]Last year in which major changes were legislated.

TABLE 7 — *Continued*

Year	Use tax	Intangibles tax	Utility property tax	Corporation fee (ACPF)
1956	33,100	22,100	17,765[a]	56,370[a]
1957	36,500	24,500	9,761	58,840
1958	36,200	25,000	20,841	64,070
1959	36,800	25,400[a]	22,352	65,700
1960	39,800	27,100	23,702	68,490
1961	43,900	29,900	25,035	70,950
1962	43,000[a]	31,700	25,166	75,410
1963	46,100	33,800	25,728	75,950
1964	50,900	34,600	26,850	82,550
1965	57,600	37,300	28,294	87,861
1966	68,600	44,200	30,701	92,766
1967	71,600	47,300	33,203	109,526

grew by only 41.6 and 59.9 percent respectively. Thus, whether measured by actual tax collections data or collections data adjusted to be consistent with the statutory rate and base provisions in a given base year, the BAT ranks high on a revenue productivity criterion, particularly from the standpoint of the ability of a tax to grow relative to the other types of levies employed by state governments.[4]

TABLE 8. Index of Collections, 1965 Rates
and Bases, 1956–1967

Year	Retail sales tax	Motor fuel tax	BAT	Cigarette tax
1956	95.4	—	88.2	91.3
1957	95.6	—	95.6	92.9
1958	92.2	—	90.2	91.3
1959	93.1	—	82.0	95.3
1960	100.0	100.0	100.0	100.0
1961	96.9	101.3	100.7	101.3
1962	99.0	104.3	94.4	105.2
1963	105.6	108.1	107.7	103.3
1964	113.0	114.3	124.4	103.0
1965	124.6	121.7	138.1	108.4
1966	136.9	130.2	164.9	112.3
1967	141.6	134.9	177.3	114.3

SOURCE: Table 7.
NOTE: 1960 = 100.

TABLE 8 — *Continued*

Year	Use tax	Intangibles tax	Utility property tax	Corporation fee (ACPF)
1956	83.1	82.0	75.0	82.3
1957	91.7	90.4	41.0	85.9
1958	91.0	92.3	87.9	93.5
1959	92.5	93.7	94.3	95.9
1960	100.0	100.0	100.0	100.0
1961	110.3	110.3	105.6	103.6
1962	108.0	116.9	106.2	110.1
1963	115.8	124.7	108.5	110.9
1964	127.9	127.7	113.2	120.5
1965	144.7	137.6	119.4	128.3
1966	172.4	163.0	129.5	135.4
1967	179.9	174.5	140.0	159.9

---

4. Although the conventional net income type levies are absent from the list of other types of taxes employed by state governments, they will be considered in the section on fiscal adequacy (pp. XX).

Annual Fluctuations

In considering the revenue productivity of the BAT, it will be useful to take a closer look at the annual yield of the levy as a revenue source. Table 9 presents the dollar collection, annual percentage change, and collection index of the BAT for the 1956–1967 period. BAT collections increased in every year except the 1957–1959 and 1960–1962 periods of national recession. As a first approximation, it appears that the BAT did vary considerably with changes in the level of business activity. In addition to its percentage decline in the recessions, the BAT recovered rapidly during the 1963–1967 recovery and growth period of the state and national economy. For example, a decline in collections of 5.7 percent in 1958 and 9.1 percent in 1959 was followed by an increase in revenues of 22 percent in 1960. Similarly, the decline in revenues in 1962 was followed by consistently large relative increases from 1963 until repeal.

TABLE 9.   Adjusted BAT Collections, 1965 Rates
and Bases, 1956–1967

Year	Collections (thousands of dollars)	Percentage change from preceding year	Index of collections (1960 = 100)
1956	63,790	—	88.2
1957	69,129	8.4	95.6
1958	65,219	–5.7	90.2
1959	59,276	–9.1	82.0
1960	72,305	22.0	100.0
1961	72,797	.7	100.7
1962	68,274	–6.2	94.4
1963	77,882	14.1	107.7
1964	89,938	15.5	124.4
1965	99,888	11.1	138.1
1966	199,221	19.4	164.9
1967	128,217	7.6	177.3

SOURCE: Table 7.
NOTE: No adjustments were made in the BAT prior to 1956 because of changes in the interstate allocation formula during those years.

Fiscal Adequacy

There has been substantial growth in state and local expenditures in recent years. The share of the nation's total output absorbed by subnational governments has increased from 6.8 percent in 1950 to

12.5 percent in 1970.[5] Consequently, much attention has been given to the capacity of state tax structures to meet the demand for increased revenues. A useful tool for evaluation of this aspect of state taxes is the measure of the income responsiveness or adequacy of tax systems.

Fiscal adequacy refers to the ability of a revenue structure to produce increasing dollar yields in order to provide for the financing of rising public service costs without frequent tax rate and/or base changes. Adequacy requires that the income elasticity of tax yields be greater than unity. If the income elasticity is less than unity — if tax yields vary in the same direction, but less than in proportion to the variation of total personal income — then the tax structure is said to exhibit revenue stability.[6]

A trade-off is necessarily established between the goals of revenue stability (income inelasticity) and adequacy (income elasticity). For example, if the state revenue structure is stable, in a period of economic expansion the relative share of income accruing to the government declines; in a deflationary period, the treasury increases its share of total income, thereby increasing its ability to command real economic resources *vis-à-vis* most other economic units. Conversely, if the revenue structure is income elastic, the state earns an increasing share of the economy's income in expansion and receives a decreasing share in deflation.

If one holds the view that in times of rising personal income the demand for public goods increases proportionately greater than the demand for private goods, and that the role of satisfying these public

---

5. U.S. Department of Commerce, Office of Business Economics, *Survey of Current Business* (Washington, D.C.: U.S. Goverment Printing Office, July 1971), Part I, p. 13; and U.S. Department of Commerce, Bureau of the Census, *Statistical Abstract of the United States: 1966* 87 (Washington, D.C.: U.S. Government Printing Office, 1966), Table 454. These figures are in current rather than real dollars. The former relationship is more meaningful when one considers that taxes are collected from current receipts.

6. A discussion of the definition and use of the adequacy concept is presented in H. M. Groves and C. Harry Kahn, "The Stability of State and Local Tax Yields," *American Economic Review* 42 (March 1952): 87–102; R. A. Musgrave, *The Theory of Public Finance* (New York: McGraw-Hill, 1959), chap. 21; James A. Papke, "Research and State Tax Reform," in *Proceedings of the Fifty-Sixth Annual Conference on Taxation* (Columbus: National Tax Association, 1963), pp. 366–70; and Harvey E. Brazer, *Taxation in Michigan: An Appraisal*, Michigan Pamphlets No. 30 (Ann Arbor: Institute of Public Administration, University of Michigan, 1961), chap. 2.

wants is properly a function of subnational governments, then it is suggested that state taxes exhibit a positive degree of income elasticity.[7] Furthermore, in order to provide for horizontal growth in public services, due to such factors as population growth and rising prices, and for vertical growth, that is, additions to the existing scope or improvements in quality of current services, the tax system must be income elastic.[8] However, if the revenue structure is stable, during economic expansion the state will find itself faced with recurrent revenue–expenditure gaps that must be met by explicit and often politically strained decisions to increase tax yields by legislating rate and/or tax base changes.

Income Responsiveness

The discussion regarding the adequacy criterion is concerned with the income elasticity of a state tax structure as a whole rather than with the income flexibility of a particular type of levy. By the very nature of the structure of state revenue systems, namely, reliance upon various levies rather than upon a single tax form, there are elements of both flexibility and inelasticity. For example, studies indicate that both the corporate net income and personal income tax meet the test of revenue adequacy. It has been estimated that the elasticity of the personal income tax will approach a coefficient between 1.4 and 1.7, whereas the corporate income tax exhibits a sensitivity coefficient of 1.5.[9] In periods of inflation or expansion, a

---

7. In a recent article, Boyle defined *fiscal imbalance* in state and local revenue–expenditure structures as the truism that the income elasticity of the revenue structure is less than that of the expenditure structure. Boyle also computes public revenue and expenditure income elasticity by type to support his argument. Gerald J. Boyle, "The Anatomy of Fiscal Imbalance," *National Tax Journal* 21 (December 1968): 412–24.

8. The single most important reason for the horizontal growth of state government expenditures can be attributed to rising prices. According to the King and Lefkowitz study, prices paid by subnational governments — especially states — rose more than twice as fast as in the private sector, and almost 25 percent faster than in the federal sector. See Donald A. King and Martin Lefkowitz, "The Finances of State and Local Governments," in *Survey of Current Business* (Washington, D.C.: U.S. Department of Commerce, Office of Business Economics, October 1967), p. 21; and Charles L. Schultze, Edward R. Fried, Alice R. Rivlin, and Nancy H. Teeters, *Setting National Priorities: The 1972 Budget* (Washington, D.C.: The Brookings Institution, 1971), chap. 6.

9. For these estimates see W. H. Waldorf, "The Responsiveness of Federal Personal Income Taxes to Income Change," in *Survey of Current Business*

state tax structure dominated by individual and business income taxation would increase its share of state product; during recession it would receive a smaller share *vis-à-vis* the rest of the economy.

On the other hand, retail sales and selective excise taxes provide a comparatively stable source of revenue due to the inclusion in the tax base of items such as food, clothing, and utilities, which have a relatively income inelastic demand.[10] Although there has been some disagreement as to the empirical estimates, the property tax, a revenue source for some state governments, also tends to have a less than unitary income elasticity.[11]

In order to estimate the income responsiveness of an entire state tax structure, computation on a weighted average of the elasticities of various components is required. If, for example, a state revenue structure relies heavily on tax sources unresponsive to income changes (such as sales and property levies), the entire structure will exhibit a low elasticity. It follows that a strong case could then be made for introducing income elastic elements (such as income taxes) into the revenue system.[12] Conversely, if an entire state tax structure

---

(Washington, D.C.: U.S. Department of Commerce, Office of Business Economics, December 1967), pp. 32–45; Wilfred Lewis, Jr., *Federal Fiscal Policy in the Postwar Recessions* (Washington, D.C.: The Brookings Institution, 1964), pp. 33–35 and 40–42; and Robert W. Rafuse, Jr., "Cyclical Behavior of State–Local Finances," in *Essays in Fiscal Federalism*, edited by Richard A. Musgrave (Washington, D.C.: The Brookings Institution, 1965), pp. 83 ff., and 83n.

10. Papke, "Research and State Tax Reform," pp. 366–67; Boyle, "Anatomy of Fiscal Imbalance," esp. pp. 412–13; and D. G. Davies, "The Sensitivity of Consumption Taxes to Fluctuations in Income," *National Tax Journal* 15 (September 1962): 287–88.

11. Groves and Kahn, and Blank indicate an income elasticity of the property tax at .22 and approximately .50 respectively, whereas Netzer and Boyle suggest coefficients of 1.00 and 0.9 respectively. Groves and Kahn, "State and Local Tax Yields," pp. 88–93; David M. Blank, "The Role of the Real Property Tax in Municipal Finances," *National Tax Journal* 7 (December 1954): esp. 319–23; and Boyle, "Anatomy of Fiscal Imbalance." For a discussion of the various estimates, see comments by Dick Netzer and Selma J. Mushkin in *Public Finances: Needs, Sources and Utilization, A Conference*, a Report of the National Bureau of Economic Research (Princeton: Princeton University Press, 1961), pp. 23–40 and 74–77 respectively.

12. Legler and Shapiro propose a model to be used as a means of determining the responsiveness of entire state revenue structures to changes in various economic variables such as per capita income, population, and tax rates. Then, on the basis of their estimating the values of elasticities, they make policy suggestions for changes in various components of the entire tax

is highly income elastic, it may be desirable to introduce elements of stability into the structure.

The Advisory Commission on Intergovernmental Relations has computed coefficients of revenue income elasticity for the fifty states, and has placed each of the states in one of three elasticity categories — low-to-medium, medium-to-high, and high. In 1967 Michigan was placed in the low-to-medium category with a coefficient of .89, the tenth most income inelastic tax structure of all the states.[13] The question is whether the BAT — the most broad-based levy of the tax system — contributed to the inelasticity of the entire Michigan structure or introduced an element of adequacy and flexibility.

Performance of the BAT

Table 10 presents the yield elasticity coefficients of the Business Activities Tax over long-term periods of six, seven, ten, and eleven years. In each case the results indicate that the BAT was more than proportionately responsive to increases in state personal income.[14]

TABLE 10. **Yield Elasticity, Selected Long-Term Periods**

Period	BAT yield elasticity coefficient
1961–67	1.25
1960–67	1.29
1956–66	1.28
1956–67	1.32

Source: Yield elasticity computed from data provided by Michigan Department of Treasury, Revenue Division; and from U. S. Department of Commerce, Office of Business Economics, *Survey of Current Business* (Washington, D.C.: Government Printing Office, selected years).

structure. See John Legler and Perry Shapiro, "The Responsiveness of State Tax Revenue to Economic Growth," *National Tax Journal* 21 (March 1968): 46–56.

13. Advisory Commission on Intergovernmental Relations, *Sources of Increased Tax Collections: Economic Growth Versus Political Choice,* Report M-41 (Washington, D.C.: U.S. Government Printing Office, 1968), p. 10.

14. For computational purposes, the formula

$$E = \frac{\triangle T/T}{\triangle Y/Y}$$

was used. The elasticity, E, measures the ratio percentage change in tax yield, T, to percentage change in state personal income, Y. Data used for the BAT was adjusted to account for discretionary rate and base changes.

However, to be relevant to the discussion regarding the goal of adequacy, that is, to provide automatic increases in revenue sufficient to meet increased demands for public goods as well as to avoid periodic legislative tax changes, it is useful to examine the record for shorter term and cyclical elasticities. Accordingly, Table 11 presents a breakdown for various two- to five-year periods. The first five periods may be classified as including recession years, and the last four, prosperity periods.[15]

TABLE 11. Income Responsiveness of Alternative
Michigan Taxes, Selected Years

Period	BAT	Corporate profit	Total business net income	Gross receipts	Tax liability
1957–60	.58	.38	.24	1.67	.60
1958–63	.74	1.49	1.40	1.53	1.31
1960–63	.54	1.21	1.35	1.17	.89
1960–64	.98	1.44	1.52	1.16	.97
1961–63	.50	1.53	1.45	1.32	1.19
1960–65	.96	1.52	1.36	.93	1.03
1962–65	1.47	1.68	1.44	.83	1.33
1963–65	1.28	1.75	1.31	.71	.84
1962–67	1.73	1.07	.92	.93	.87
1965–67	1.91	.37	.33	1.07	.35

SOURCES: Estimates computed from Michigan Department of Treasury, Revenue Division, *Annual Report* (Lansing: the Department, various years); Daniel B. Suits, *Econometric Model of Michigan*, Technical Report No. 3 (Lansing: Michigan Department of Commerce, 1966); Harvey E. Brazer et al., *General Fund Estimates of Revenues and Expenditures to 1975* (Lansing: Michigan Department of Commerce, 1967); U.S. Department of Treasury, Internal Revenue Service, *Statistics of Income: Business Income Tax Returns* (Washington, D.C.: Government Printing Office, selected years); and Advisory Commission on Intergovernmental Relations, *State and Local Fiscal Capacity and Tax Effort*, Report M-16 (Washington, D.C.: Government Printing Office, 1962).

The results indicate that during periods of expansion the BAT exhibited a high coefficient of elasticity, ranging from 1.28 to 1.91 for the years presented. On the other hand, during the periods 1957–1960 and 1961–1963 the BAT exhibited various degrees of stability. This switch from stability to income elasticity can largely be explained by recalling that the major components of the BAT base

15. The cyclical classifications are based on data in U.S. Department of Commerce, Bureau of the Census, *Business Conditions Digest* (selected issues); and Rendigs Fels and C. Elton Hinshaw, *Forecasting and Recognizing Business Cycle Turning Points* (New York: National Bureau of Economic Research, 1968), chaps. I-4, I-5, and I-6.

were payroll and profit. Payrolls tend to rise at least proportionately with income during expansionary periods (especially if the state, as is Michigan, is characterized by strong labor unions with cost-of-living clauses in contracts), and tend to decline less than total income in recession. In addition, business profits tend to over-recover in expansions. As a result, a tax such as the BAT will be more responsive to income increases than to declines.[16]

Table 11 presents the coefficients of income responsiveness of alternative hypothetical broad-based business tax levies available to Michigan. This permits comparison of the adequacy of the BAT *vis-à-vis* the other more conventional state tax levies (corporate profits, all business net income, gross receipts, and federal-plus-state tax liability).

In general, the BAT was more stable than the profits or net income type measures. Indeed, except for the 1962–1967 and 1965–1967 periods, the elasticity coefficient of the BAT was consistently less than that of the profit-based levies. It is well to note that these results are consistent with the behavior of payrolls and profits during cyclical fluctuations. A further investigation reveals that during expansion the BAT would be more responsive to changes in personal income than would a tax on business gross receipts or a piggyback state tax on taxable business income, whereas in deflationary periods the BAT exhibits relative fiscal stability.

Examination of BAT collections over time suggests that the tax met the test of revenue adequacy, and, as a result, added an important element of flexibility to the Michigan tax revenue structure during times of economic growth. In addition, although the BAT was less income elastic than the hypothetical net income levy, it had a characteristic of revenue stability during periods of recession. It met the adequacy criterion during economic expansion, but was stable for the downturns, a feature which highly recommends its form as an element in a state revenue structure.[17]

---

16. Lewis, *Federal Fiscal Policy,* pp. 33, 53.

17. The BAT is not unique in the characteristic of exhibiting different income elasticities during expansions and contractions. For example, the individual income tax is more flexible, albeit still income elastic, during contractions than expansions. See Lewis, *Federal Fiscal Policy,* esp. pp. 38–45.

6

Impact Analysis
Part I: Payments by
Type of Business

A general business tax such as the BAT is legally defined as a comprehensive tax to be levied on some measure of activity of all businesses regardless of size, industrial organization, or legal classification, but there are practical, legal, political, and institutional considerations which often result in a narrowing of the base to which the tax actually is applied. Although the BAT was to be levied on "all business activities in or caused to be engaged within the state [of Michigan], whether in intrastate, interstate or in foreign commerce," it does not follow that, in practice, the tax reached all business groups.[1]

Accordingly, the impact of the Michigan BAT is analyzed in order to identify the extent to which different business groups actually paid the tax. This analysis will provide an historical perspective of the BAT, will identify the source of the major structural defects, and

---

1. Act 150, P. A. 1953, Sec. 205.551 (e) as amended.

will present the resultant professional criticism of the BAT.[2]

Impact versus Incidence

The concept of tax impact as opposed to tax incidence is of concern in this study. In the terminology of taxation, the *impact* of a tax refers to the legal monetary obligation of the initial taxpaying unit. That unit passes or shifts the tax either forward to consumers in the form of higher product prices, or backward to its factors through a reduction in prices paid for inputs. Then the tax obligation is on individuals, and there results a change in the personal distribution of income. This latter effect of the tax on individuals is the *incidence* of the tax.[3] The two concepts are related, but are distinctly separate issues; and although the importance of examining a business tax for its ultimate incidence effects on individuals is not to be minimized, it is the impact of a particular levy which is of concern in a business tax study.

In particular, the following five points may be made to support the contention that it is the impact of the BAT which warrants attention. First, an examination of incidence deals with the effects of tax policy on the personal distribution of income. That aspect refers to people, not things such as businesses. For a tax jurisdiction operating in essentially a closed economy framework, and thus able to control factor mobility and overspill (externality) benefits of its budget policy, a recourse to the expedient of nonpersonal taxation in order to achieve policy objectives is not necessary.

However, because states operate in open economies, and therefore

---

2. For example, see remarks by Leo Mattersdorf, "Suggested Changes in Michigan's Tax Structure," in *Taxes and Economic Growth*, pp. 143–44; and Richard E. Slitor, "The Role of Value Added Taxation in the Tax Structure of the States: Prospective Developments," in *Proceedings of the Sixty-First Annual Conference on Taxation* (Columbus: National Tax Association, 1968), pp. 107–15.

3. There is an abundance of literature dealing with the topic of tax impact and incidence. For a survey and discussion of this literature see the following sources: Ursula Hicks, *Public Finance* (New York: Pitman Publishing Company, 1947); Peter Mieszkowski, "Tax Incidence Theory: The Effects of Taxes on the Distribution of Income," *Journal of Economic Literature* 7 (December 1969): 1103 ff.; Musgrave, *Theory of Public Finance*, pp. 211–31; and Donald Phares, "Equity in State–Local Taxation: An Interstate Analysis," in *Proceedings of the Sixty-Fourth Annual Conference on Taxation* (Columbus: National Tax Association, forthcoming).

have no direct control over either factor mobility or overspill benefits, using business as a tax collecting intermediary may be the only procedure available for assessing individuals, wherever they may reside, for the benefits of state services which initially accrue to the business firm. As a result, it is the issue of the impact of a business tax (over which the state has direct control through its various statutory provisions), and not the incidence on resident and nonresident incomes (over which a state has only a marginal effect through its tax structure), which warrants attention for the analysis of a state business levy such as the BAT.

Second, issues in the debates regarding structural equality of business taxation among industries, inputs, and site locations — of particular importance in open economies due to the characteristic of factor mobility — are primarily those of tax impact analysis. This may be particularly true in a situation in which a state's major industries are producing primarily for export purposes, that is, for sales in an out-of-state market.

Third, even though numerous studies have concluded that state tax costs are a relatively minor element in total business costs and in industial location decisions,[4] businessmen maintain that state tax levels must be considered in making managerial decisions. Similarly, in tax policy decision making state legislatures constantly express concern about state "tax climate" or "image," and often the policy discussions focus on issues of state business tax structure and tax costs and burdens on industry.[5] To the extent that such issues of business taxation play a role in private and public discussions, it is the impact approach which is relevant.

Finally, there are two practical justifications for concentrating on the impact rather than the incidence approach in business taxation: (1) due to the present state of the art regarding the theory of tax shifting in the open economy, there is no meaningful alternative to a direct impact analysis; and (2) even if the theory of business tax shifting were empirically operational, the impact determination would be a prerequisite to any further discussions about tax incidence.

---

4. For a review of these studies see John F. Due, "Studies of State–Local Tax Influences on Location of Industry," *National Tax Journal* 14 (June 1961): 163–73.

5. For example, see Advisory Commission on Intergovernmental Relations, *State–Local Taxation and Industrial Location*, Report A-30 (Washington, D.C.: U.S. Government Printing Office, 1967), chap. 4.

The primary importance of the impact approach in business tax matters is justified on its own merits due to reasons of practical tax policy considerations and because it is the only way to measure the valid tax cost element in subnational business operations.[6]

Nature and Limitations of the Analysis

In spite of their usefulness, impact studies are subject to qualitative and quantitative misinterpretation. The major analytical–qualitative limitations should be mentioned.

• With the exception of data relating to tax payment by legal form of business organization, the impact analysis here employs a cross-sectional rather than a time-series approach. Although various relationships among taxpayer classifications may be established for a given representative year, it does not necessarily follow that these relationships are the same over time. However, the use of a cross-sectional method is useful as a means for focusing specifically on various structural aspects of business taxes. Although a year-by-year analysis could be considered as a method of allowing one to examine and contrast the effects of various statutory changes on the distributional pattern of a particular tax, the time-series approach also has the great disadvantage of unavoidably incorporating in the measures unique cyclical stabilization aspects of each particular year.[7]

• An impact study is concerned with tax *levels* and tax *structures*, not with the question of whether or not a particular tax type is acceptable in principle. That a tax on business activity conform to various administrative, compliance, and welfare criteria principles is an important consideration in the appraisal of state tax policy. In-

6. The tax cost concept is based on the proposition that the supply of government services which accrues to business constitutes a fifth factor of production. Thus, just as payroll expenditures are a factor cost attributed to the labor input, taxes are a factor cost paid to government.

7. The representative year chosen for this study was 1965. This period was characterized in Michigan by a fully employed (3.5 percent unemployment) and price-stable economy (the consumer and wholesale price index rose 1.7 and 1.9 percent respectively). In addition to the favorable stabilization aspects, 1965 is also a good benchmark year for this study since all major statutory changes in the BAT had been made by that time. Data sources: Daniel B. Suits, *Econometric Model of Michigan,* Technical Report No. 3 (Lansing: Michigan Department of Commerce, 1966), Table A-9; and U.S. Department of Labor, Bureau of Labor Statistics, Bulletin No. 1600 (Washington, D.C.: U.S. Government Printing Office, 1968).

deed, many of the discussions on value-added taxation have been focused on the issue of the proper rationale for subnational business taxation. Tax impact studies are of little use if the particular form of tax under examination is considered a violation of various accepted qualitative tax principles.

• Since the purpose of impact analysis is to make an examination of the relative structural effect on industrial groups, no attention is given to the height of the statutory rate of taxation. This aspect of tax policy can have practical political importance since tax levies are often judged by legislators and lobbyists on the basis of level of tax rate rather than on one of definition (breadth) of the taxable base itself.

• Finally, this analysis focuses first on the impact of the BAT, and then on the impact of the BAT *vis-à-vis* various alternative, equal yield, broad-based business taxes. Because there is no appraisal of the total state (or state-plus-local) tax impact on business, the combined impact of various local and other state levies, that is the total business tax package, is not considered.

Distribution of Tax Payments

Business Activities Tax collection data for different business legal organizations by percentage of the total number of BAT taxpayers, and by percentage of total tax paid, are presented in Tables 12 and 13 respectively. During the last decade of the tax, the years after the major statutory amendments had been added to the original 1953 act, corporate taxpayers paid an average of 69 percent of total collections, yet accounted for only 25 percent of the total number of taxpayers. In contrast, Michigan's sole proprietorships and partnerships generally accounted for more than 70 percent of the number of taxpayers, but paid, on the average, less than 13 percent of total collections.

The relationship between the size of tax payment and the number of taxpayers is presented for a single year in Table 14. It can be observed that the bulk of the BAT receipts were paid by large taxpayers. To illustrate, for 1967 less than 2 percent of the total taxpayers filing — those in the $5,000 and above tax due categories — paid more than 64 percent of the total tax due. The importance of the contribution of large taxpayers to total BAT collections is further illustrated by the fact that 95 firms, less than 1 percent of the total number of taxpayers, paid more than 41 percent of the total tax bill. Conversely, 61 percent of the taxpayers paid less than 1 percent of the total tax yield for that year. The relative importance of the large taxpayers is also demonstrated by the fact that the 25 largest Michigan BAT taxpayers contributed more than 35 percent of the total tax due.[8]

TABLE 12.   Percentage of Number of BAT Taxpayers Reporting, by Ownership, Selected Years

Year	Sole proprietorship	Partnership	Corporation	Other	Total
1956	53.6	23.0	20.1	3.3	100.0
1959	50.9	23.4	21.7	4.0	100.0
1961	49.7	22.7	24.2	4.4	100.0
1963	48.6	22.1	25.6	3.7	100.0
1964	45.1	21.0	29.8	4.6	100.0
1965	46.0	20.6	28.8	4.6	100.0
1966	46.2	20.6	28.7	4.5	100.0
1967	45.3	20.3	28.8	5.6	100.0

SOURCE: Michigan Department of Treasury, Revenue Division, *Annual Report* (Lansing: the Department, 1956–1967).

TABLE 13.   Percentage of Total BAT Paid, by Ownership, Selected Years

Year	Sole proprietorship	Partnership	Corporation	Other	Total
1956	15.5	6.5	63.5	14.5	100.0
1959	8.4	6.6	65.7	19.3	100.0
1961	6.8	5.5	66.7	21.0	100.0
1963	6.8	5.5	69.3	18.4	100.0
1964	6.1	4.6	70.4	18.9	100.0
1965	5.9	4.4	70.9	18.8	100.0
1966	5.8	4.2	72.5	17.5	100.0
1967	6.1	4.1	70.0	19.8	100.0

SOURCE: Michigan Department of Treasury, Revenue Division, *Annual Report* (Lansing: the Department, 1956–1967).

8. This figure was estimated from 1967 BAT returns made available from the Revenue Division of the Michigan Department of Treasury and by the Office of the Director of the State Budget. A further breakdown of this data is not possible because of disclosure agreements.

TABLE 14. BAT Collections, by Size of Payment, 1967

Tax paid (in dollars)	Number of taxpayers	Percentage of taxpayers	Cumulative percentage of taxpayers	Tax paid (in dollars)	Percentage of tax paid	Cumulative percentage of tax paid
No tax paid	56,635	42.07	42.07		.00	.00
0.01 – 99.99	25,781	19.15	61.22	1,161,524	.96	.96
100.00 – 249.99	18,988	14.11	75.33	3,116,058	2.58	3.54
250.00 – 499.99	12,694	9.43	84.76	4,498,855	3.73	7.27
500.00 – 999.99	8,952	6.65	91.41	6,290,515	5.22	12.49
1,000.00 – 4,999.99	9,136	6.79	98.20	18,884,270	15.66	28.15
5,000.00 – 9,999.99	1,254	.93	99.13	8,815,280	7.31	35.46
10,000.00 – 24,999.99	713	.53	99.66	11,088,790	9.19	44.65
25,000.00 – 49,999.99	242	.18	99.84	8,203,265	6.80	51.45
50,000.00 – 99,999.99	120	.09	99.93	8,247,706	6.84	58.29
100,000.00 – over	95	.07	100.00	50,304,873	41.71	100.00
Subtotal	134,610	100.00		120,611,138	100.00	
Refunds and adjustments				7,606,223	.00	
Total	134,610	100.00		128,271,361	100.00	

SOURCE: Adapted from Michigan Department of Treasury, Revenue Division, *Annual Report* (Lansing: the Department, 1967).
NOTE: Details may not add to totals due to rounding.

TABLE 15. BAT Collections, by Industrial Origin, 1955–1967, All Returns

Year	Agriculture		Mining		Manufacturing		Utilities		Wholesale trade	
	Thousands of dollars	Percentage composition	Thousands of dollars	Percentage composition	Thousands of dollars	Percentage composition	Thousands of dollars	Percentage composition	Thousands of dollars	Percentage composition
1955	34	.1	178	.6	12,562	41.9	695	2.3	1,372	4.6
1956	49	.1	442	.7	32,617	54.9	1,108	1.9	2,556	4.3
1957	71	.1	290	.5	38,744	60.2	1,320	2.1	3,427	5.3
1958	76	.1	409	.7	36,153	59.5	1,290	2.1	2,908	4.8
1959	85	.2	386	.7	31,346	56.7	1,197	2.2	2,858	5.1
1960	86	.1	360	.5	43,477	60.1	1,589	2.2	3,435	4.8
1961	106	.1	458	.6	43,857	60.3	1,178	1.6	3,389	4.7
1962	96	.1	497	.7	41,541	60.8	1,720	2.5	3,114	4.6
1963	145	.2	488	.6	48,200	61.9	1,865	2.4	3,432	4.4
1964	146	.2	626	.7	57,350	63.8	1,874	2.1	4,070	4.5
1965	182	.2	710	.7	62,731	62.8	2,111	2.1	4,568	4.6
1966	219	.2	889	.8	75,544	63.4	2,275	1.9	5,324	4.5
1967	254	.2	877	.7	78,357	61.1	2,510	2.0	6,769	5.3

TABLE 15 — Continued

Year	Retail trade Thousands of dollars	Percentage composition	Services Thousands of dollars	Percentage composition	Professional Thousands of dollars	Percentage composition	Other Thousands of dollars	Percentage composition	All industry Thousands of dollars	Percentage composition
1955	4,939	16.5	3,354	11.2	342	1.1	6,500	21.7	29,976	100.0
1956	9,465	15.9	12,197	20.5	648	1.1	366	.6	59,448	100.0
1957	10,642	16.5	8,853	13.8	835	1.3	134	.2	64,316	100.0
1958	10,294	17.0	8,679	14.3	852	1.4	66	.1	60,727	100.0
1959	10,272	18.5	8,321	15.0	886	1.6	65	.1	55,326	100.0
1960	11,519	15.9	10,732	14.8	1,034	1.4	74	.1	72,305	100.0
1961	12,277	16.9	10,367	14.2	1,105	1.5	59	.1	72,797	100.0
1962	11,050	16.2	9,081	13.3	1,110	1.6	63	.1	68,274	100.0
1963	12,438	16.0	9,879	12.7	1,345	1.7	88	.1	77,882	100.0
1964	12,858	14.3	11,388	12.7	1,441	1.6	185	.2	89,938	100.0
1965	14,409	14.4	13,351	13.4	1,630	1.6	196	.2	99,888	100.0
1966	16,665	14.0	16,119	13.5	1,938	1.6	249	.2	119,222	100.0
1967	17,960	14.0	18,940	14.8	2,136	1.7	414	.3	128,217	100.0

SOURCE: Michigan Department of Treasury, Revenue Division, *Annual Report* (Lansing: the Department, 1955–1967).
NOTE: Details may not add to totals due to rounding

Cross-Industry Impact

Data on the dollar amount of tax collections and the percentage distribution of these collections by Michigan industrial groups for the entire life of the BAT are presented in Table 15. The record emphasizes the dominance of Michigan manufacturing as a source of BAT collections. Although manufacturing constituted less than 10 percent of the total number of registered taxpayers, it contributed the major share of BAT collections, an average of 59 percent for the ten-year period.[9]

The importance of the manufacturing sector is further indicated by the fact that it consistently paid almost 80 percent of BAT revenue derived from firms which owed $5,000 or more in tax.[10] That manufacturing was the major contributor to the BAT follows from the relative importance of the industry in the economic base of Michigan (more than 47 percent of the state's gross product originates in manufacturing), and from the practical effect of the combination of the minimum standard deduction and the specific dollar exemption, which eliminated many small manufacturing and nonmanufacturing businesses from the taxable base. On the basis of the information in this chapter it can be concluded that although, by legal definition, the tax was applied to all business, the major share of the tax was paid by large corporate manufacturing business.

---

9. Table 15 presents tax payment data by the industrial grouping as presented in all the issues of the *Annual Report* of the Michigan Department of Treasury. In the classification breakdown, Michigan included the construction industry, but not professionals, as part of the service industry. Thus, the services category takes on a much greater quantitative importance in the Michigan *Annual Report* data than would be true if the U.S. Bureau of the Budget's Standard Industrial Classification (SIC) were used to define industries. The SIC method is used for all subsequent industrial data.

10. Michigan Department of Treasury, Revenue Division, *Annual Report*, 1957–67.

7

Impact Analysis
Part II: Interindustry
Differentials

The identification of tax levels will not provide sufficient information for policy makers who must choose a particular method of business taxation. Another question, that of determining interindustry
tax structure, that is, a comparative analysis of the cost or burden
effects of various business taxes, is now being viewed by state tax
economists as critical to tax policy matters.[1] Interindustry structural
tax differentials can directly affect the business tax policy decisions
of state legislators, even in the absence of information regarding its
effects.

> The question of the "proper" method of taxing industry is one of the
> thorniest confronting state government fiscal decision makers. On
> the one hand, the potentially large revenue yield of the direct busi-
> ness tax is welcomed by the fiscally pressured state government; but
> on the other, there are the ever-present fears that high taxes will

---

1. John B. Legler and James A. Papke, "Toward a Rationalization of
State–Local Business Taxation," in *Proceedings of the Fifty-Eighth Annual Conference on Taxation* (Columbus: National Tax Association, 1965), p. 541.

drive industry from the state, or at least cause it to stop expanding. As a consequence of the former, proposed state tax reform more often than not centers around some adjustment to the state business tax structure. As a consequence of the latter, the success of such proposed reform, in the state legislature, often turns on the potential or believed effects on the state's industry. This continues to be true, even in the face of a great volume of research which indicates with more than a little consistency that taxes play only a minor role in the location decisions of industry.[2]

A number of Michigan tax reform studies called for repeal of the BAT, based, in part, on the issue of its structural equity or neutrality.[3] Accordingly, the issue of structure is relevant to an analysis of the Michigan experience with value-added type taxation. The inter-industry structural effects of the actual BAT *vis-à-vis* both hypothetically modified BAT levies and alternative state business tax forms will be analyzed by means of differential impact analysis — an examination of the relative distribution of tax liabilities associated with the substitution of equal yield taxes.

Indices of Structural Equality

Identification of economic neutrality or structural tax differences among various industry classifications is a crucial question for a study of business tax policy, since the choice of a particular index of comparison will tend to predetermine the answer as to the proper method of taxing business.[4] One way to measure tax liability differences is to

---

2. Roy W. Bahl and Kenneth L. Shellhammer, "Fiscal Planning and State Business Taxation: An Application of Input-Output Analysis," in *Proceedings of the Sixty-First Annual Conference on Taxation* (Columbus: National Tax Association, 1968), p. 418.

3. However, no study measured these structural tax inequalities among tax-paying groups. For example, see Alfred G. Buehler, "The State and Local Tax Structure and Economic Development," and Leo Mattersdorf, "Suggested Changes," both in *Taxes and Economic Growth*, p. 42 and p. 144. Also see comments by Howard Preston, "The Michigan Business Activities Tax as Viewed by Small Businessmen," in *Proceedings of the Forty-Eighth Annual Conference on Taxation* (Columbus: National Tax Association, 1955), pp. 34–35.

4. In the context of business taxation, *neutrality* refers to the equal treatment of business units in similar circumstances, but economists may legitimately disagree on what these particular circumstances are. As used in this chapter, *neutrality* will refer to the same tax treatment among industries according to some predetermined index of equality among industries. In order to avoid a confusion of terms (*neutrality* is also used to refer to resource

relate industry tax collection information to appropriate economic data common to all business activities. This method provides a common denominator for comparison of the interindustry impact of a tax, and permits analysis of the degree of structural tax equality among taxpayer groups. A number of business and economic statistics have been suggested for use as an index of equality measure as a basis for such comparisons. Among these are: business net income, gross receipts, capital investment, payroll size, number of employees, population, personal income originating in business, and value added or some similar measure of income or product originating. Depending on the purpose of the analysis, each of the indices has some merit.

Business Net Income

Business net income, or profit, is frequently employed to make tax burden comparisons among industrial classes.[5] The use of this statistic as a measure of structural equality can be justified if one accepts two assumptions: that the business firm as an institutional entity has some sort of ability to pay or taxpaying capacity that is separate from its stockholders or other types of factor owners; and that general business tax obligations will be paid out of operating profits, that is, reductions in the returns to the firm's owners (stockholders or individual partners and proprietors) and not in reduced payments to other factor owners (for example, wages to labor).

However, if the general taxation of business is justified on the grounds that business firms receive government services regardless

---

allocation effects of taxes), this equal treatment among industries will be referred to as *structural tax equality*. For a discussion of the application of this concept of equality (equity, neutrality) see Dick Netzer, *Economics of the Property Tax* (Washington, D.C.: The Brookings Institution, 1966), chap. 2; James A. Papke, "The Taxation of Business Enterprise," pp. 559–69; and E. B. Schmidt, "Determining Structural Tax Inequalities among Business Firms," *Nebraska Journal of Economics and Business* 2 (Spring 1962): 29–31. Schmidt's discussion is not restricted to general business taxes but includes all state and local taxes paid by business firms.

5. For a recent example, see Arthur D. Little, Inc., *Hawaii's General Excise Tax: Prospects, Problems and Prescriptions*, a Report to the State of Hawaii Department of Taxation (Honolulu: 1968), pp. 26–27. The use of the word *burden* connotes tax collections from individuals and not institutions such as business firms. However, for convenience and convention, it will be used in this study to refer to the ratio of a business tax payment to a firm's net income.

of the level of profits, then net income–profits is deficient as an index. This measure fails to consider that certain types of businesses, as a result of organizational operation, differences in input mixes, or the degree of managerial efficiency, may realize small, zero, or even negative profits. Although such firms receive government services and may pay nonprofit based taxes, they are excluded from the profit measure of structural equality.

To illustrate a defect of profit as a structural equality index, assume two firms, A and B, are alike, with one exception. Both have equal adjusted receipts bases and each receive the same amount of government services, but firm A's adjusted receipts base is computed as the sum of $25,000 of property, $55,000 of labor, and $15,000 of profits, and firm B's adjusted receipts are the sum of $25,000 property, $45,000 labor, and $25,000 profits. The BAT tax due for both firms equals $736.25, but for A the structural tax impact ratio is 5.91 percent and for B it is 2.94 percent. This rather large structural tax inequality is due solely to the fact that the firms have different input mixes, and the profits index reflects this difference.

Similarly, a situation could be illustrated on the basis of managerial efficiency differences among firms or industries. Assume that two businesses are alike in all respects including organizational function and input mix, except that one of the firms has lower profits than the other due to poor management techniques. With profits as the index of equality, the same conclusion regarding structural tax inequality could be reached — with the same qualitative defects.

Nevertheless, if one accepts the two assumptions noted at the beginning of this discussion, then profits, at least in the short run, can be used as a structural measure for a business's capacity to pay taxes. This is true even if one considers the type of objections illustrated above. From the ability or capacity point of view, low profit levels by definition indicate low taxpaying capacity and the structural tax inequalities that result are the measure that is desired.

Gross Receipts

The merit of gross receipts as the index of equality among different types of business is that it includes in the denominator all operating firms which receive government services regardless of profitability. However, the gross receipts measure has a serious defect. Just as the use of profits implicitly measures such qualitative aspects as managerial efficiency or variability of input mix, the gross receipts measure does not adjust for variation in the degree of vertical integration. For example, for a firm which is completely vertically integrated through final distribution of gross receipts, the gross monetary value of the final product equals the sum of value added at each stage of production. If the same product were produced by separate businesses, the sum of 'gross receipts beyond the first stage of production would be greater than value added due to the inclusion of interfirm purchases. Thus, the size of a tax paid–gross receipts ratio would decline for successive stages of production as the degree of vertical integration decreases.

Capital Investment

The use of capital investment as a measure of the structural index of equality can be justified if business taxes are viewed as a form of property taxation, or as a reduction in the private rate of return from investment. With either view, the use of capital investment would be an acceptable index of equality among various different industry classifications. However, the capital investment ratio has a shortcoming similar to that of any one-factor measure: it ignores the fact that there are other factors of production, and that the mix of these factors varies among industry classes.[6]

Payrolls, Employees, and Production

Tax impact measures such as the ratio of taxes paid to payroll data, number of employees, and production per worker man-hours also have been employed in various tax studies to identify structural tax inequalities. These could be justified on the assumptions that labor productivity measures reflect the business contribution of all the factors of production and that they are easily computed. Nevertheless, such measures have the same conceptual defects regarding the production input mix issue as do the profits and capital investment measures. For example, in the case of payrolls or number of employees,

---

6. The property factor still is sometimes used. A 1959 Wisconsin state tax impact study employed farm real estate value as the appropriate denominator for farm tax payments due. The rationale for the measure was "the importance of property taxation to the farming industry." University of Wisconsin Tax Study Committee, *Wisconsin's State and Local Tax Burden* (Madison: University of Wisconsin Press, 1959), pp. 22–23.

ceteris paribus, the ratio measure overemphasizes tax impact on non-labor intensive industries.[7]

Personal Income

The use of personal income originating as an index is justified on the grounds that ultimately all tax payments are made from personal income as it is received as factor payments, or as it is spent for consumption purposes. Such a view is not without merit, and in an analysis of the effect of a business tax on individuals, for example, by income classes, there is some reason to employ an income flow received measure as an index of equality among taxpayers. However, an income flow concept broader than personal income originating is preferable for a business impact analysis.

Value Added

Value added measures the net dollar contribution to total state product by the business enterprise. As such, it approximates the sum of returns to the factors of production (the total dollar cost of business activity). The ratio of tax payment to value added may be employed as an index of tax costs, that is, the relative importance of the tax in the total cost structure of the firm.[8]

---

7. *Wisconsin's State and Local Tax Burden* employed these measures for the analysis of the manufacturing tax impact (pp. 14–19, Table 6). It must be noted here that the purpose of the Wisconsin study was to compare *interstate* tax impact differentials and not *intrastate* industry distributions. When employing such statistics as number of employees, payrolls, and personal income originating in business, comparisons were drawn between states for the same industries. For example, in comparing Wisconsin and Michigan tax impact on farming, real estate values were used, and when analyzing manufacturing, tax due per employee was used. Although the conceptual defects of measures such as payroll exist, an issue such as the interindustry input mix is not so crucially relevant to the Wisconsin work.

8. Since value added measures the total dollar cost of business activity, the ratio of tax payments to value added will determine the size of tax costs. The Advisory Commission on Intergovernmental Relations used personal income derived from business activity as a common denominator for comparing the relative weight of business taxes. The measure was used as a "second best index" because of the absence of business GNP estimates by states. See the commission's *State Taxation and Industrial Location,* p. 66 ff. The Michigan gross state product measure used in this study solves that problem. Dick Netzer, *Economics of the Property Tax,* p. 26, adopts value added as the yardstick for appraisal of taxes by industry group.

Value added also permits interindustry comparisons with an index of equality which automatically adjusts for variations in (1) combination of factors of production (a criticism of the profit, capital, and labor measures), (2) degree of vertical integration (unlike the gross receipts measure), and (3) market organization (a particular defect of the profits and gross receipts standards).[9]

Choosing an Index

A rather obvious and most important characteristic of an analysis of measures of cross-industry structural tax inequalities is that the choice of the index will tend to predetermine the degree of structural variation among the types of businesses. If net income is chosen as the index, profits taxes will exhibit the smallest degree of interindustry structural inequality. Similarly, if the net income variant of value added is selected that type of tax would exhibit the least structural variation among the industry classifications. The choice of the denominator index will, by definition, determine which tax form is the most equitable. This is not to suggest that the tax cost and burden measures are of no use. On the contrary, they permit both separate industrial groups and state policy makers to examine relative tax structure relationships which otherwise would not be possible, but caution is required in the interpretation of the results.

One final characteristic of structural tax relationships should be mentioned. The estimates of the constructed tax data were based on the implicit assumption that all business receipts would be attributed to Michigan, and took no explicit account of apportionment of interstate receipts to other states. Yet tax liability depends on apportionment as well as on the statutory definition of a tax base, and the dollar tax cost and the industry variations of the BAT may, in fact, be affected by the apportionment approach used under the law.[10]

With these limitations in mind, two interindustry measures have been employed in this study for purposes of comparative analysis: net income and the gross state product variant of value added.[11] By using both of these, one not only can identify variations in the

---

9. See Schmidt, "Determining Structural Tax Inequalities," p. 31. This argument applies to total state and local tax comparisons as well as to a general business tax.

10. The tax liability effects of various apportionment formulas are discussed in chapter 8.

11. See footnote 8, this chapter.

TABLE 16.   Actual BAT Payments and BAT Payments as a Percentage of Gross State Product and Net Income, by Industry, 1965

Industry	Actual BAT collections (thousands of dollars)	Distribution (percentage)	Percentage of gross state product	Index[a]	Percentage of net income	Index[a]
Agriculture	182	0.2	.03	7.7	.11	5.5
Mining	710	0.7	.28	71.8	1.80	90.0
Construction	5,453	5.5	.48	123.0	3.07	153.5
Manufacturing	62,731	62.8	.47	120.5	2.24	112.0
Utilities	2,111	2.1	.08	20.5	.51	25.5
Wholesale trade	4,568	4.6	.25	64.1	1.89	94.5
Retail trade	14,409	14.4	.45	115.4	2.99	149.5
Services	9,528	9.5	.33	84.6	1.42	71.0
Other	196	0.2	(NA)	—	(NA)	—
All industry*	99,888	100.0	.39	100.0	2.00	100.0

SOURCES: Computed from tax return data (1965) supplied by Michigan Department of Treasury, Revenue Division; U.S. Department of Treasury, Internal Revenue Service, *Statistics of Income: Business Income Tax Returns* (Washington, D. C.: Government Printing Office, 1965); Daniel B. Suits, *Econometric Model of Michigan*, Technical Report No. 3 (Lansing: Michigan Department of Commerce, 1966); and Harvey E. Brazer et al, *General Fund Estimates of Revenue and Expenditures to 1975*, Technical Report No. 11 (Lansing: Michigan Department of Commerce, 1967).

NOTE: Details may not add to totals due to rounding.

(NA): Not available.

[a] All-industry average equals 100.0.

relative tax burden and tax cost positions of industry, but also can provide measures consistent with the two conventionally divergent views of the taxpaying nature of the business entity. These views are that taxes are not a cost of production and, therefore, should be imposed only on the profitable firm, or that taxes are an element of overall economic production costs (payments to all factors including government), and should be levied on all firms regardless of the level of profitability.

Measuring Structural Impact

Data for Michigan BAT payments in 1965 by the nine major Standard Industrial Classification (SIC) groups are presented in Table 16. The percentage distribution of the actual cross-industry dollar tax amount due indicates manufacturing paid the bulk of the BAT. However, on the basis of the ratio of this tax collections data to various indices of equality among industries, the structural impact of the tax was quite different. For example, on the basis of the gross state product index it can be seen that construction, manufacturing, and retailing all had a relatively high measure of tax impact in terms of tax costs. Alternatively, the BAT imposed a comparatively lower tax cost on the agricultural, mining, wholesale trade, and service trade classifications.

If business tax policy objectives dictate that tax cost neutrality among various industry groups be achieved, that is, that there be equality among the tax payment–value-added ratios for industries, then the BAT was markedly non-neutral, and some modifications in the tax structure were needed. Indeed, within the context of the tax cost index these structural tax inequalities were substantial. To illustrate, construction, manufacturing, and retail trade not only had the largest BAT costs, but also were the only industries ranked above the hypothetical all-industrial average tax cost of .39 percent.[12]

---

12. The all-industry averages of structural tax impact ratios are weighted, not unweighted, figures. Rather than make the benchmark (100.0) equal to a simple arithmetic mean of the sum of each of the separate industry groups divided by the number of industries, the average is computed by dividing the total yield by the total base. As a result, a relative importance is assigned to each industry in proportion to its importance in the state economic base. To illustrate, had the unweighted figure been used as the benchmark in column 4 of Table 16, the average would have been 29.6 = 100.0. This would give undue emphasis to agriculture (ratio = .08), would greatly

Although some tax cost structural inequalities would inevitably result from the need to choose among the alternative estimates, the differences in columns 3 and 4 of Table 16 are primarily due to the special low rate treatment for utilities, the inconsistent statutory treatment of depreciation, and the practical effect of the combination of the minimum standard deduction and specific dollar exemptions.[13]

On the basis of a net income or tax burden measure, the impact was also greatest for construction, but retail trade, not manufacturing, was second. In terms of manufacturing's ranking *vis-à-vis* construction and retail trade and its relation to the all-industry tax burden figure, the impact on manufacturers is considerably reduced when the burden rather than the cost index is employed. On the other hand, the groups which were low tax cost industries, namely, agriculture, utilities, services, and mining, also had the lowest effective BAT burden.

Because of the great quantitative importance of the role of the manufacturing sector in the Michigan economy, the tax cost and burden impact measures were computed for thirteen manufacturing classifications (Table 17).[14] The state's transportation equipment industry, which accounts for the bulk (43.9 percent) of total Michigan value added by manufacturing, incurred the greatest tax impact in terms of both cost and burden measures. Five other manufacturing classes — food products, paper products, primary metals, chemicals, and furniture and fixtures — which together accounted for a quarter of the state's value added, were also above the total manufacturing tax cost and burden averages. However, since cross-industry differences in type of general business organizations and in

increase the index of manufacturing (from 120.5 to 158.7), and would put mining at the average tax rank rather than below the all-industry average. The numbers achieved by the simple calculating process are the same which would result from the longer process of weighting each index number by its respective contribution to gross product or net income.

13. It is of interest to note that these sources of tax cost structural inequalities are deviations of the BAT from the concept of pure value-added taxation.

14. In 1965 Michigan's manufacturing accounted for more than 47 percent of total gross state product. One subclassification — transportation equipment — constituted nearly 20 percent of the total state output. Those classifications which contributed less than 1.25 percent of Michigan value added by manufacturing were included in the "Other manufacturers" category. Sources: Suits, *Econometric · Model for Michigan*, pp. 13–35, 41; and U.S. Department of Commerce, Bureau of the Census, *Annual Survey of Manufacturers* (Washington, D.C.: U.S. Government Printing Office, 1964 and 1965), pp. 243–45.

TABLE 17. BAT Payments as a Percentage of Gross State Product and Business Net Income, by Manufacturer, 1965

Manufacturer	Percentage of gross state product (GSP)	Index[a]	Percentage of net income	Index[a]
Food and kindred products	.48	102.1	2.28	101.8
Furniture and fixtures	.51	108.5	2.39	106.7
Paper and allied products	.48	102.1	2.27	101.3
Printing and publishing	.42	89.4	1.97	87.9
Chemicals and allied products	.49	104.3	2.31	103.1
Rubber and plastics	.41	87.2	1.96	87.5
Stone, clay, and glass	.39	83.0	1.86	83.0
Primary metal	.48	102.1	2.28	101.8
Fabricated metal	.42	89.4	1.97	87.9
Machinery, except electrical	.44	93.6	2.05	90.6
Electrical machinery	.43	91.5	2.03	90.6
Transportation equipment	.53	112.8	2.51	112.1
Other	.46	97.9	2.16	96.4
Total	.47	100.0	2.24	100.0

SOURCES: Computed from tax return data (1965) supplied by Michigan Department of Treasury, Revenue Division; U.S. Department of Treasury, Internal Revenue Service, *Statistics of Income: Business Income Tax Returns* (Washington, D.C.: Government Printing Office, 1965); U.S. Department of Commerce, Bureau of Census, *Annual Survey of Manufacturers: 1965* (Washington, D.C.: Government Printing Office, 1968); Daniel B. Suits, *Econometric Model of Michigan*, Technical Report No. 3 (Lansing: Michigan Department of Commerce, 1966); and Harvey E. Brazer et al., *General Fund Estimates of Revenue and Expenditures to 1975*, Technical Report No. 11 (Lansing: Michigan Department of Commerce, 1967).

[a] All-industry average equals 100.0.

input–output functions were less significant than the differences which characterize various major industry groups, the quantitative structural tax inequalities within manufacturing were much smaller than the inequalities between major industry classes.[15]

Measuring Cross-Industry Differentials

In order to quantitatively examine the cross-industry effects of modifying the actual BAT levy by eliminating the particular statutory provisions which are the major deviations of the BAT from a pure value-added tax, four alternative state business taxes will be contrasted. The comparison will be made for equal total yield taxes in order to focus on the details of the reordering of the tax distributional patterns by industry which would result from various tax law changes. Using this technique the following general business taxes will be examined:[16] actual BAT collections; an adjusted receipts tax like the BAT except that the preferential utilities rate and the standard deduction and specific dollar exemption provisions are elimi-

---

15. This quantitative fact serves as an example that the defects of various indices of equality proposed for measuring structural tax equalities are more serious when used for interindustry than intraindustry measures of equality. It also indicates that the reasons for observed structural tax impact differences within major industry sectors may occur due to factors different from those explaining major cross-industrial inequalities. For example, for reasons often not immediately obvious (other than ease of compliance or reluctance to disclose the firm's business data to a state tax office), many of the largest taxpayers elected to use the 50 percent minimum standard deduction *in lieu* of the itemization of deductions in computing adjusted receipts. As a result, the industry sector with which these firms are identified would tend to have a higher tax base, and, therefore, tax due, than that sector characterized by firms which generally elected to itemize and take legitimate deductions in excess of 50 percent of gross receipts.

16. The only actual data are for the BAT. All other tax data were estimated since the Michigan tax jurisdiction did not employ the other business taxes. As a consequence, the BAT data reflect the effect of various discretionary tax base erosions, while the other taxes are more comprehensive. Only the actual BAT includes the effects of minimum deduction and specific dollar exemption provisions. It is quite possible that had any of the substitute taxes been adopted in Michigan similar erosions to the tax base might have occurred. Granting this assumption, the most meaningful comparisons in the following section would be to contrast the adjusted receipts tax (as the representative BAT form) with the value-added, gross receipts, and income tax levies. Data collection and construction methodology is discussed in Appendix C.

TABLE 18. Payments and Distribution, Alternative BAT Bases, by Industry, 1965

Industry	Actual BAT		Adjusted receipts tax		Adjusted receipts less total depreciation		Adjusted receipts less depreciation and depletion	
	Thousands of dollars	Percentage composition	Thousands of dollars	Percentage composition	Thousands of dollars	Percentage composition	Thousands of dollars	Percentage composition
Agriculture	182	0.2	1,595	1.6	1,397	1.4	1,416	1.4
Mining	710	0.7	644	0.6	622	0.6	498	.5
Construction	5,453	5.5	5,094	5.0	5,228	5.2	5,302	5.3
Manufacturing	62,731	62.8	62,961	63.0	63,792	63.9	63,444	63.5
Utilities	2,111	2.1	7,936	7.9	7,312	7.3	7,393	7.4
Wholesale trade	4,568	4.6	4,173	4.2	4,255	4.3	4,306	4.3
Retail trade	14,409	14.4	8,504	8.5	8,485	8.5	8,606	8.6
Services	9,528	9.5	8,885	8.9	8,744	8.8	8,901	8.9
Other	196	0.2	96	0.2	53	—	22	—
All industry	99,888	100.0	99,888	100.0	99,888	100.0	99,888	100.0

SOURCES: Computed from tax return data (1965) supplied by Michigan Department of Treasury, Revenue Division; U.S. Department of Treasury, Internal Revenue Service, *Statistics of Income: Business Income Tax Returns* (Washington, D.C.: Government Printing Office, 1965); Daniel B. Suits, *Econometric Model of Michigan*, Technical Report No. 3 (Lansing: Michigan Department of Commerce, 1966); and Harvey E. Brazer et al., *General Fund Estimates of Revenue and Expenditures to 1975*, Technical Report No. 11 (Lansing: Michigan Department of Commerce, 1967).

nated; an adjusted receipts less depreciation tax exactly like the adjusted receipts levy except that the former permits a deduction for personal property depreciation in addition to real property depreciation; and an adjusted receipts tax which permits depletion as well as total depreciation allowances.

The focus of this section is not on the conceptual reasons for the modification of the BAT, but on the tax impact of these alternative BAT type levies, and on any change in the structural tax inequalities which would result from the elimination of the aforementioned statutory provisions (Table 18). Once the BAT base is modified by the elimination of the standard deduction and specific dollar exemption, and by the application of a uniform rate on all industry groups, the tax payments for agriculture, utilities, and manufacturing increase, although the last change is rather small (0.2 percent). All other industry groups (notably retailing) have a lower tax obligation. The effect of the elimination of the dual rate scheme alone is as would be expected: on an equal yield basis all groups, other than utilities, experience an absolute decrease in tax due.[17]

Since the practical effect of the specific dollar exemption was to entirely relieve small businesses from the burden of the tax, elimination of this provision, *ceteris paribus*, would increase the amount of tax due from those industries which included a large number of small operations. In Michigan the two industries with the largest number of small taxpayers were agriculture and manufacturing.[18] The results of the elimination of the specific dollar exemption are reflected in the adjusted receipts tax column of Table 18.[19]

---

17. A dollar comparison of the BAT with actual dollar figures on an equal yield basis for the utility rate adjustment was computed, but is not separately presented here.

18. Sources: U.S. Department of Commerce, Bureau of the Census, *U.S. Census of Business*, vol. 1, *Retail Trade Area Statistics*, Part 1; vol. 4, *Wholesale Trade* (Washington, D.C.: U.S. Government Printing Office, 1966); and Department of Treasury, Internal Revenue Service, *Business Tax Returns* (Washington, D.C.: U.S. Government Printing Office, 1966), Tables 2.3, 2.4, 3.3, 3.4, 5.5, 5.6. It is of interest to note that the Michigan farm lobby was primarily responsible for obtaining the specific dollar exemption provision. See remarks by Donald K. Barnes, "The Anomalous Michigan Business Activities Tax," p. 116.

19. There are two explanations for the large reduction in tax payments by retail trade. First, retail trade is characterized by a high deductions–gross receipts ratio. The removal of the 50 percent minimum deduction provision would increase the tax due for industries having a low deductions–gross receipts ratio (agriculture, construction, mining, utilities, services) and

Unlike the specific exemption, a minimum standard deduction does not affect the number of firms reporting, but merely reduces the tax base against which statutory rates are applied. By eliminating this provision in the BAT law, the tax base for each industry is increased by the difference between the size of the standard deduction and the amount of itemized deductions. As a practical matter, the ratio of itemized deductions to gross receipts was, on the average, greater than 50 percent for all major industry groups except agriculture and services.[20] Once the change has been made from the actual BAT to the adjusted receipts form of the tax, the percentage distribution of tax payments by industry group is only slightly affected by the further change of permitting deductions for personal property depreciation and depletion allowance. The construction, manufacturing, and wholesale trade sectors increase in relative importance when this latter distribution is computed on an equal yield basis.

Tables 19 and 20 present the tax cost and tax burden estimates for measuring the interindustry structural tax differences for alternative equal yield BAT and modified BAT levies. The modification of the actual BAT to the adjusted receipts tax clearly would reduce the degree of cross-industry structural tax inequality, indicated by the fact that the range of the variance of the index numbers from the all-industry average is much smaller for the adjusted receipts levy.

Whereas most of the other industry groups are relatively unchanged, agriculture and, of course, utilities have a much higher tax cost and burden; there are two primary reasons. First, with the elimination of the combination of the specific dollar exemption and the minimum deduction, some businesses previously excluded from the tax would become registered taxpayers. If such businesses are a relatively large part of the total industrial sector, the tax ratio numerator increases substantially, which is the case for agriculture. Second, when industry gross state product and net income figures are used as denominators in the impact ratios, these numbers implicitly include the respective aggregate value of all firms (taxpaying plus nontaxpaying) in the particular industry category. In the actual BAT measure tax payments were made only by those firms having gross receipts greater than $25,000 per year. Consequently, the ratio of the

---

therefore reduce the payments of retail trade. Second, data in column 1 of Table 18 are based on Michigan Department of Treasury codes, and include firms classified as retailers which were not similarly identified under U.S. Budget Bureau SIC coding (columns 2–4).

20. See chapter 9.

TABLE 19. **Payments as a Percentage of Gross State Product, Alternative Equal Yield BAT Bases, 1965**

Industry	Actual BAT		Adjusted receipts tax		Adjusted receipts less total depreciation		Adjusted receipts less depreciation and depletion	
	Percentage	*Index*[a]	*Percentage*	*Index*[a]	*Percentage*	*Index*[a]	*Percentage*	*Index*[a]
Agriculture	.03	7.7	.25	78.1	.23	74.2	.23	74.2
Mining	.28	71.8	.25	78.1	.24	77.4	.20	64.5
Construction	.48	123.0	.45	140.6	.46	148.4	.47	151.6
Manufacturing	.47	120.5	.48	150.0	.48	154.8	.48	154.8
Utilities	.08	20.5	.32	100.0	.29	93.5	.29	93.5
Wholesale trade	.25	64.1	.23	71.9	.24	77.4	.24	77.4
Retail trade	.45	115.4	.26	81.3	.26	83.9	.27	87.1
Services	.33	84.6	.31	96.9	.30	96.8	.31	100.0
All industry	.39	100.0	.32	100.0	.31	100.0	.31	100.0

Sources: Computed from tax return data (1965) supplied by Michigan Department of Treasury, Revenue Division; U.S. Department of Treasury, Internal Revenue Service, *Statistics of Income: Business Income Tax Returns* (Washington, D.C.: Government Printing Office, 1965); Daniel B. Suits, *Econometric Model of Michigan*, Technical Report No. 3 (Lansing: Michigan Department of Commerce, 1966); and Harvey E. Brazer et al., *General Fund Estimates of Revenue and Expenditures to 1975*, Technical Report No. 11 (Lansing: Michigan Department of Commerce, 1967).

[a] All-industry average equals 100.00.

TABLE 20. Payments as a Percentage of Business Net Income,
Alternative Equal Yield BAT Bases, 1965

Industry	Actual BAT		Adjusted receipts tax		Adjusted receipts less total depreciation		Adjusted receipts less depreciation and depletion	
	Percentage	Index[a]	Percentage	Index[a]	Percentage	Index[a]	Percentage	Index[a]
Agriculture	.11	5.5	1.00	55.2	.91	51.1	.92	52.0
Mining	1.80	90.0	1.63	90.1	1.58	88.8	1.26	71.2
Construction	3.07	153.5	2.86	158.0	2.94	165.2	2.98	168.4
Manufacturing	2.25	112.0	2.24	123.8	2.27	127.5	2.26	127.7
Utilities	.51	25.5	1.93	106.6	1.78	100.0	1.80	101.7
Wholesale trade	1.89	94.5	1.73	95.6	1.72	96.6	1.78	100.6
Retail trade	2.99	149.5	1.77	97.8	1.76	98.9	1.79	101.1
Services	1.42	71.0	1.34	72.9	1.30	73.0	1.33	75.1
All industry	2.00	100.0	1.81	100.0	1.78	100.0	1.77	100.0

Sources: Computed from tax return data (1965) supplied by Michigan Department of Treasury, Revenue Division; U.S. Department of Treasury, Internal Revenue Service, *Statistics of Income: Business Income Tax Returns* (Washington, D.C.: Government Printing Office, 1965); Daniel B. Suits, *Econometric Model of Michigan*, Technical Report No. 3 (Lansing: Michigan Department of Commerce, 1966); and Harvey E. Brazer et al., *General Fund Estimates of Revenue and Expenditures to 1975*, Technical Report No. 11 (Lansing: Michigan Department of Commerce, 1967).
[a] All-industry average equals 100.00.

actual payments to the denominators is proportionately greater for those industries which, in general, did not have a relatively large number of businesses excluded from the tax base (such as manufacturing, wholesale and retail trade), and correspondingly lower for industries which were the principal beneficiaries of the combined provisions (such as agriculture, mining, and construction).

Despite all the modifications in the tax base, the manufacturing structural tax ratios changed relatively little. This indicates that the industry, although it had a large number of small firms, was heavily weighted by large taxpayers, and, as a result, manufacturing was essentially unaffected in terms of tax due or in size of denominators when the standard deduction and specific dollar exemption provisions were eliminated. The practical effect on interindustry relationships of the last two modifications (which permitted the deductibility of personal property and depletion allowances) would have been to markedly reduce the tax cost and burden to mining (primarily because of the depletion allowance) and, to a lesser extent, to agriculture and utilities. Other industry groups would have been relatively unaffected by the changes. In fact, on this equal yield comparison the deduction of personal property depreciation would have had a surprising practical effect, since the retailing industry would have received no tax cost trade-off benefits, but would have experienced a slight increase in tax burden. This would occur in spite of the fact that it was the retailer's lobby which was most positively concerned with legislation permitting the widened depreciation deduction treatment.[21]

Alternative Levies

In order to focus on relative cross-industry tax distribution patterns, an examination of the interindustry distributional pattern of tax payment, cost, and burden measures for six substitute Michigan general business taxes is presented. Data is on an equal yield basis (1965 BAT yield). The six substitute taxes are: (1) the BAT with a single adjustment made to eliminate the preferential rate afforded utilities; (2) the adjusted receipts tax from Table 18; (3) a net income value-added tax; (4) a levy on gross business receipts; (5)

---

21. See remarks by Stephenson, "The Michigan Business Activities Tax," pp. 29–33; and Barnes, "The Anomalous Michigan Business Activities Tax," pp. 116–17.

a total business (sole proprietorship, partnership, and corporate) net income tax; and (6) a corporation net income tax.

Distribution of Tax Bases

The distribution of alternative tax liabilities by industrial classifications is presented in Table 21. The importance of manufacturing for all six types of taxes is clearly evident; its share ranges from nearly 75 percent under the corporate income tax levy to 54 percent under the gross receipts tax. Although manufacturing's share is large under the corporation net income tax, its relative tax liability falls by 20 percentage points if the net income tax base is defined to include all businesses.

Changes in percentage of total tax paid for the other industry groups are less pronounced except for trade-orientated industries, which would experience an increased tax payment obligation under gross receipts levies relative to the other taxes in Table 21. This result is not surprising since only a gross receipts tax disallows deductions for all interfirm purchases. Since the ratio of interfirm purchases to receipts is largest for retail and wholesale trade relative to the other industrial groups, it follows that inclusion of interfirm purchases in the tax base would increase trade-orientated industry tax payments.[22]

Tax Payments and Costs

The Michigan tax cost ratios of tax payments to gross state product by various industrial groups are presented in Tables 22 and 23. For each of the substitute taxes, except the corporation net income levy, tax payment figures were divided by total business gross product by industry type. The corporation income tax payments were divided by a corporate (not total) gross product base. The reason for this special treatment is that if a tax is defined as corporate only, a meaningful common denominator index of structural equality must reflect that definition. Since the business activities, adjusted receipts, value-added, gross receipts, and total net income taxes are all levied on total business, the cost index should be total business. Similarly, a tax on corporations only is related to a corporate measure only.

Two kinds of information can be analyzed on the structural tax

---

22. See chapter 9.

TABLE 21. Payments under Alternative Equal Yield Taxes, by Industry, 1965

Industry	BAT		Adjusted receipts tax		Value-added tax		Gross receipts tax		Net income tax		Corporate net income tax	
	Thousands of dollars	Percentage composition	Thousands of dollars	Percentage composition	Thousands of dollars	Percentage composition	Thousands of dollars	Percentage composition	Thousands of dollars	Percentage composition	Thousands of dollars	Percentage composition
Agriculture	170	.2	1,595	1.6	1,528	1.5	1,376	1.4	3,192	3.2	264	.3
Mining	668	.7	644	.6	612	.6	433	.4	790	.8	948	.9
Construction	5,119	5.2	5,094	5.0	5,023	5.0	4,271	4.3	3,562	3.6	1,624	1.6
Manufacturing	58,920	59.2	62,961	63.0	62,109	62.2	53,933	54.0	56,197	56.3	74,660	74.7
Utilities	8,180	7.7	7,936	7.9	7,818	7.8	5,079	5.1	8,228	8.2	10,296	10.3
Wholesale trade	4,289	4.3	4,173	4.2	4,385	4.4	12,459	12.5	4,835	4.8	4,364	4.4
Retail trade	13,535	13.6	8,504	8.5	9,390	9.4	17,390	17.4	9,632	9.6	5,399	5.4
Services	8,915	9.0	8,858	8.9	8,994	9.0	4,513	4.5	13,432	13.5	2,317	2.3
Other	92	.1	96	.1	29	—	434	.4	23	—	16	—
All industry	99,888	100.0	99,888	100.0	99,888	100.0	99,888	100.0	99,888	100.0	99,888	100.0

Sources: Computed from tax return data (1965) supplied by Michigan Department of Treasury, Revenue Division; U.S. Department of Treasury, Internal Revenue Service, *Statistics of Income: Business Income Tax Returns* (Washington, D.C.: Government Printing Office, 1965); Daniel B. Suits, *Econometric Model of Michigan*, Technical Report No. 3 (Lansing: Michigan Department of Commerce, 1966); Harvey E. Brazer et al., *General Fund Estimates of Revenue and Expenditures to 1975*, Technical Report No. 11 (Lansing: Michigan Department of Commerce, 1967); and National Planning Association, Center for Economic Projections, *State Projections to 1975*, Report No. 65-II (Washington, D.C.: the Association, 1965).

Note: Details may not add to totals due to rounding.

cost (or burden) data of the alternative levies: the relative tax liability position of a given industry compared to other industrial classifications, and the relative tax cost (or burden) of a single industry under the various substitute taxes. Among the major industrial classifications, the manufacturing and construction industries would pay the highest tax costs for all three of the value-added type levies (BAT, adjusted receipts, or net income variant of value added). With a gross receipts or total net income based tax, manufacturing and construction would have had reduced tax costs, and, conversely, the wholesale trade, agricultural, and (for the net income tax) service industries would have had higher cost rankings among industries.

The tax cost trade-off by a given major industry under the alternative taxes can be seen by reading across the data in Table 22. To cite an example, the lowest tax cost for manufacturing would be a gross receipts levy, the highest the corporate income tax; the same is true for utilities and mining. Retailers, however, have the opposite range relationship.

The quantitative importance of manufacturing to Michigan justifies a further breakdown by manufacturing industries. Accordingly, intraindustry tax cost distributions and the trade-offs for each industry under the alternative levies were estimated in Table 23. Due to the similarity of structural industrial organization, the intraindustry variations in tax cost are less pronounced than they are across major industry categories.

Tax Payments and Burden

The ratios of industry tax payments to net income are given in Tables 24 and 25. As was true for the tax cost measures, the denominators for the first five taxes in each of the tables are computed for total business, whereas the corporate net income levy burden figure is computed from corporation data only. Since the denominator of these industry tax burden ratios, by definition, is the business net income measure, it follows that the industry ratios will be equal to the rate applied to the appropriate total business or corporate net income base (2.00 and 2.76 percent respectively) which would yield the same amount of total revenue as the other taxes under consideration. Complete structural tax burden equality among industry groups, therefore, is achieved for the net income measures. As a result, the most interesting comparisons of the data in Table 24 and 25 are the horizontal relationships, or the relative tax burden measures within each industry category for the alternative levies.

TABLE 22. Payments as a Percentage of Gross State Product, Alternative Equal Yield Taxes, by Industry, 1965

Industry	BAT		Adjusted receipts tax		Value-added tax		Gross receipts tax		Net income tax		Corporate net income tax	
	Percentage	Index[a]	Percentage	Index[a]	Percentage	Index[a]	Percentage	Index[a]	Percentage	Index[a]	Percentage	Index[a]
Agriculture	.03	9.7	.25	78.1	.25	78.1	.22	62.9	.51	137.8	.32	82.1
Mining	.26	83.9	.25	78.1	.24	75.0	.17	48.6	.31	83.7	.43	110.3
Construction	.45	145.2	.45	140.6	.44	137.5	.38	108.6	.32	86.5	.21	53.8
Manufacturing	.44	141.9	.48	150.0	.47	146.8	.41	117.1	.42	113.5	.58	148.7
Utilities	.33	106.5	.32	100.0	.31	96.9	.20	57.1	.33	89.2	.43	110.3
Wholesale trade	.24	77.4	.23	71.9	.24	75.0	.69	197.1	.27	73.0	.30	76.9
Retail trade	.42	135.5	.26	81.3	.29	90.6	.54	154.2	.30	81.1	.28	71.8
Services	.31	100.0	.31	96.9	.31	96.9	.16	45.7	.47	127.0	.19	48.7
All industry	.31	100.0	.32	100.0	.36	100.0	.35	100.0	.37	100.0	.39	100.0

SOURCES: Table 21; Daniel B. Suits, *Econometric Model of Michigan*, Technical Report No. 3 (Lansing: Michigan Department of Commerce, 1966); Harvey E. Brazer et al., *General Fund Estimates of Revenue and Expenditures to 1975*, Technical Report No. 11 (Lansing: Michigan Department of Commerce, 1967); and National Planning Association, Center for Economic Projections, *State Projections to 1975*, Report No. 65-II (Washington, D.C.: the Association, 1965).

NOTE: 1965 BAT yield equals $99,888,000.

[a] Each all-industry average equals 100.0 for the particular tax. Data were rounded in obtaining separate industry index numbers.

TABLE 23. Payments as a Percentage of Gross State Product, Alternative Equal Yield Taxes, by Manufacturer, 1965

Manufacturer	BAT		Adjusted receipts tax		Value-added tax		Gross receipts tax		Net income tax		Corporate profit tax	
	Percentage	Index[a]	Percentage	Index[a]	Percentage	Index[a]	Percentage	Index[a]	Percentage	Index[a]	Percentage	Index[a]
Food and kindred products	.48	102.1	.48	100.0	.48	102.1	.35	85.3	.22	53.7	.31	53.4
Furniture and fixtures	.41	108.5	.52	108.3	.53	112.8	.27	65.9	.22	53.7	.31	53.4
Paper and allied products	.48	102.1	.51	106.3	.48	102.1	.28	68.3	.27	65.8	.35	60.3
Printing and publishing	.42	89.4	.44	91.7	.44	93.6	.22	53.7	.25	61.0	.34	58.6
Chemicals and allied products	.49	104.3	.49	102.1	.48	102.1	.26	63.4	.41	100.0	.56	96.6
Rubber and plastics	.41	87.2	.42	87.5	.41	87.2	.29	70.7	.22	53.7	.30	51.7
Stone, clay, and glass	.39	83.0	.42	87.5	.40	85.1	.24	58.5	.26	63.4	.36	62.1
Primary metal	.48	102.1	.49	102.1	.47	100.0	.29	70.7	.30	73.2	.41	70.7
Fabricated metal	.42	89.4	.42	87.5	.42	89.4	.31	75.6	.26	63.4	.36	62.1
Machinery, except electrical	.44	93.6	.45	93.8	.44	93.6	.25	61.0	.34	82.9	.47	81.0
Electrical machinery	.43	91.5	.42	87.5	.42	89.4	.30	73.1	.24	58.5	.33	56.9
Transportation equipment	.53	112.8	.52	108.3	.52	110.6	.41	100.0	.51	124.4	.69	119.0
Other	.46	97.9	.47	97.9	.46	98.0	.29	70.7	.29	70.7	.40	69.0
Total	.47	100.0	.48	100.0	.47	100.0	.41	100.0	.41	100.0	.58	100.0

Sources: Table 21; Daniel B. Suits, *Econometric Model of Michigan*, Technical Report No. 3 (Lansing: Michigan Department of Commerce, 1966); Harvey E. Brazer et al, *General Fund Estimates of Revenue and Expenditures to 1975*, Technical Report No. 11 (Lansing: Michigan Department of Commerce, 1967); National Planning Association, Center for Economic Projections, *State Projections to 1975*, Report No. 65-II (Washington, D.C.: the Association, 1965); and U.S. Department of Commerce, Bureau of Census, *Annual Survey of Manufacturers: 1965* (Washington, D.C.: Government Printing Office, 1968), pp. 243–45.
[a] Index of collections. All-industry average equals 100.0.

A comparison of the adjusted receipts and the value-added tax with the total business net income tax shows that only for manufacturing and construction would the tax burden decrease under the net income approach. All other industries would experience increases in tax burden ratios (see Table 24). The same kind of tax burden relationships are evident in the manufacturing breakdown in Table 25. To illustrate, assume that the 1967 Michigan legislature had decided to reform the BAT to an adjusted receipts tax rather than to replace it with a corporate-plus-noncorporate net income levy. If the assumption is made that various businessmen would support the approach that gave them the lowest tax burden, then almost all the manufacturers would have opposed that change.[23]

A Policy Application

Earlier in this chapter it was asserted that tax structure effects, known or supposed, can be a crucial determinant of tax policy decisions. Accordingly, data were constructed to measure the structural tax cost and burden effects of a number of alternative tax levies, ranging from reforming the BAT to replacing it. Two kinds of information can be obtained from this data: the structural tax cost and burden effects among and within industries under the various tax approaches.

The first of these, the variations of tax cost or burden ratios among industry groups, is of interest from a policy viewpoint. If, for example, various types of taxes are rated for structural tax equality or inequality characteristics on the basis of the variations of individual industry measures from the all-industrial tax cost average (that is, sum of the various industry dispersions from the average), then the taxes with the largest structural tax cost inequalities are, respectively, the gross receipts, corporate net income, and the actual BAT levies. On the other hand, the total net income, value-added, and adjusted receipts tax levies have a much smaller interindustry tax cost variation.

Thus, if a primary objective of the Michigan business tax system was to achieve structural tax cost equality among industry groups, then the logical decision would have been either to reform the BAT to make it conform to a net income type value-added levy, or to replace it altogether with a net income tax on all business activity.

---

23. Recall that it is relative comparisons which are important here. The height of the tax burden (or cost) measure is a function of the amount of (equal) revenue yield used in constructing all the industry tax estimates.

TABLE 24. Payments as a Percentage of Business Net Income, Alternative Equal Yield Taxes, by Industry, 1965

Industry	BAT		Adjusted receipts tax		Value-added tax		Gross receipts tax		Net income tax		Corporate Net income tax	
	Percentage	Index[a]	Percentage	Index[a]	Percentage	Index[a]	Percentage	Index[a]	Percentage	Index[a]	Percentage	Index[a]
Agriculture	.11	6.0	1.00	55.2	.96	52.7	.90	.42	2.00	100.0	2.76	100.0
Mining	1.69	92.1	1.63	90.1	1.55	85.2	1.10	.52	2.00	100.0	2.76	100.0
Construction	2.87	156.4	2.86	158.0	2.82	154.9	2.40	1.13	2.00	100.0	2.76	100.0
Manufacturing	2.10	114.5	2.24	123.8	2.21	121.4	1.92	.90	2.00	100.0	2.76	100.0
Utilities	1.99	108.5	1.93	106.6	1.90	104.4	1.24	.58	2.00	100.0	2.76	100.0
Wholesale trade	1.77	96.5	1.73	95.6	1.82	100.0	5.16	2.42	2.00	100.0	2.76	100.0
Retail trade	2.81	153.2	1.77	97.8	1.95	107.1	3.62	1.70	2.00	100.0	2.76	100.0
Services	1.33	72.5	1.34	72.9	1.33	73.1	.67	.31	2.00	100.0	2.76	100.0
All industry	1.83	100.0	1.81	100.0	1.82	100.0	2.13	100.0	2.00	100.0	2.76	100.0

SOURCES: Computed from tax return data (1965) supplied by Michigan Department of Treasury, Revenue Division; U.S. Department of Treasury, Internal Revenue Service, *Statistics of Income: Business Income Tax Returns* (Washington, D.C.: Government Printing Office, 1965); Daniel B. Suits, *Econometric Model of Michigan*, Technical Report No. 3 (Lansing: Michigan Department of Commerce, 1966); and Harvey E. Brazer et al, *General Fund Estimates of Revenue and Expenditures to 1975*, Technical Report No. 11 (Lansing: Michigan Department of Commerce, 1967).

NOTE: 1965 BAT yield equals $99,888,000.

[a] All-industry average equals 100.0. Data were rounded in obtaining separate industry index numbers.

TABLE 25. Payments as a Percentage of Business Net Income, Alternative Equal Yield Taxes, by Manufacturer, 1965

Manufacturer	BAT		Adjusted receipts tax		Value-added tax		Gross receipts tax		Net income tax		Corporate profit tax	
	Percentage	Index[a]	Percentage	Index[a]	Percentage	Index[a]	Percentage	Index[a]	Percentage	Index[a]	Percentage	Index[a]
Food and kindred products	2.28	101.8	2.30	102.7	2.29	103.6	1.67	87.0	2.00	100.0	2.76	100.0
Furniture and fixtures	2.39	106.7	2.47	110.3	2.52	114.0	1.30	67.7	2.00	100.0	2.76	100.0
Paper and allied products	2.27	101.3	2.38	106.3	2.28	103.2	1.33	68.3	2.00	100.0	2.76	100.0
Printing and publishing	1.97	87.9	2.08	93.0	2.09	94.6	1.05	54.7	2.00	100.0	2.76	100.0
Chemicals and allied products	2.31	103.1	2.30	102.7	2.26	102.3	1.20	63.0	2.00	100.0	2.76	100.0
Rubber and plastics	1.96	87.5	1.99	88.8	1.96	88.7	1.38	71.9	2.00	100.0	2.76	100.0
Stone, clay, and glass	1.86	83.0	2.00	89.3	1.91	86.4	1.13	58.6	2.00	100.0	2.76	100.0
Primary metal	2.28	101.8	2.30	102.7	2.23	100.9	1.38	71.8	2.00	100.0	2.76	100.0
Fabricated metal	1.97	87.9	1.96	87.5	1.98	89.6	1.45	75.5	2.00	100.0	2.76	100.0
Machinery, except electrical	2.05	91.5	2.12	94.6	2.07	93.7	1.16	60.4	2.00	100.0	2.76	100.0
Electrical machinery	2.03	90.6	1.99	88.8	1.98	89.6	1.42	74.0	2.00	100.0	2.76	100.0
Transportation equipment	2.51	112.1	2.46	109.8	2.44	110.4	1.96	102.1	2.00	100.0	2.76	100.0
Other	2.16	96.4	2.19	97.3	2.17	98.2	1.37	71.4	2.00	100.0	2.76	100.0
Total	2.24	100.0	2.24	100.0	2.21	100.0	1.92	100.0	2.00	100.0	2.76	100.0

Sources: Computed from tax return data (1965) supplied by Michigan Department of Treasury, Revenue Division; U.S. Department of Treasury, Internal Revenue Service, *Statistics of Income: Business Income Tax Returns* (Washington, D.C.: Government Printing Office, 1965); U.S. Department of Commerce, Bureau of Census, *Annual Survey of Manufacturers: 1965* (Washington, D.C.: Government Printing Office, 1968); Daniel B. Suits, *Econometric Model of Michigan*, Technical Report No. 3 (Lansing: Michigan Department of Commerce, 1966); and Harvey E. Brazer et al., *General Fund Estimates of Revenue and Expenditures to 1975*, Technical Report No. 11 (Lansing: Michigan Department of Commerce, 1967).

[a] All-industry average equals 100.0.

8

Taxation of

Interstate Business

The method of taxation of interstate (or multistate) business by various state tax jurisdictions is a critical factor in determining the merits of a particular state business tax policy. State governments operate in open economies, that is, there is no tax jurisdictional authority to erect tariffs or other barriers to commerce, nor to control movements of final products, services, and labor and capital resources across boundaries. Consequently, a mechanism must be established to determine what fraction of a business firm's total tax base (net income, gross receipts, adjusted receipts, value added, and so forth) is attributable to a particular jurisdiction. Although there is wide agreement that multistate business activity should be subject to state tax, there has been a notable lack of agreement as to approach.[1]

---

1. A significant step in the direction of uniformity in state taxation of interstate business has been made with the development of the multistate Tax Compact. The Compact, which has developed guideline legislation for states as of January 1972 has been adopted by 21 legislatures. For a discussion, see George Kinnear, "The Multistate Tax Commission: A New Experiment in Intergovernmental Relations," *Canadian Tax Journal* 19 (March–April 1971): 136–43; and Commerce Clearing House, "State Tax News," *Taxes* 49 (March through May, July, and November 1971): 189; 253; 318; 443; 711.

Indeed, the method chosen for apportionment of adjusted receipts was one of the most controversial features of the Michigan Business Activities Tax, and, as a result of this single issue, it was widely predicted that the Michigan courts would declare the BAT inapplicable to multistate business activity.[2]

Apportionment of interstate receipts is important both to the businesses being taxed and to the taxing jurisdiction.[3] For government, the issue of interstate apportionment has serious revenue productivity implications because the courts recognize that no state may levy business taxes on an unapportioned or unallocated tax base, and because the particular choice of apportionment method, by definition, determines the size of the aggregate tax base. For business, there are obvious tax cost effects and issues of structural tax inequality between a particular firm (or industry) and its competitors. In addition, both business and government administrators agree that certain methods for apportioning receipts are, as a practical matter, unacceptable from a tax compliance standpoint.

The Conceptual Framework

The conceptual issues of the interstate division of the tax base are given only summary consideration in the following discussion.[4] How-

---

2. Lock, Rau, and Hamilton, "The Michigan Value Added Tax," p. 361. This legal attack is made in Paul Kauper and Samuel Estep, "Interstate Transactions," pp. 11–22. However, in a case involving an Ohio corporation doing business partially in Michigan, the Michigan Supreme Court upheld the legality of the BAT as an income tax on interstate commerce. See discussion in chap. 4.

3. The imposition of a tax on an unallocated or unapportioned base violates the commerce clause of the *U.S. Constitution. Western Union Tel. Co.* v. *Kansas ex. rel* Coleman, 216 U.S. 1 (1910). An unapportioned tax also violates the due process clause. For discussion, see Walter H. Beaman, *Paying Taxes to Other States* (New York: Ronald Press, 1963), p. 3-2.

4. This matter has been adequately covered elsewhere: Beaman, *Paying Taxes to Other States;* Charles E. Ratliff, Jr., *Interstate Apportionment of Business Income for State Income Tax Purposes* (Chapel Hill: University of North Carolina Press, 1962); *State Taxation of Interstate Commerce,* Report of the Special Subcommittee on State Taxation and Interstate Commerce of the Committee on the Judiciary, House of Representatives, 88th Cong., 2d sess. (1964), 4 vols., see esp. vol. 1, Part II; "Interstate Taxation of Business," in *Proceedings of the Sixty-Second Annual Conference on Taxation* (Columbus: National Tax Association, 1969), pp. 604–30. McLure recently has focused on the conceptual aspects in a subnational context: Charles E.

ever, of special concern is the BAT's treatment of the interstate business firm and the effect of alternative apportionment formulas on state revenues and taxpayer impact. There are three fundamentally different solutions to the problem of apportionment of multistate business receipts: separate ,accounting, specific allocation, and formula apportionment.

Separate Accounting

Separate accounting permits a business firm to treat its operations in different states as if they were separate and distinct value-creating activities. If a business adopts this approach, it must organize its bookkeeping as if each of its state operations were a separate business with its own receipts, profits, balance sheets, and income statements (including all items which appear in these accounts).

This approach is a reasonable one if, in fact, each state operation represents a separate activity from a home office or center of business activity (for example, various franchise operations). However, the rationale of separate accounting breaks down when the activities of a business are too small to be computed separately, or when profits and receipts or certain expenses (for example, management, capital costs) are realized in a central consolidated statement. In addition, the case for separate accounting is further weakened when various interstate intraplant services and expenses are made which require arbitrary allocation of plant costs. As a result of these defects separate accounting is of limited use and, in general, is restricted to those business enterprises which can prove to the appropriate state tax agency that alternative methods do not fairly represent the extent of the taxpayer's business activity in the state.[5]

Specific or Direct Allocation

A second method of apportionment, specific or direct allocation, is provided by most states as an optional means of division of the tax

---

McLure, Jr., "The Value Added Tax and State and Local Finance," in *Proceedings of the Sixty-Fourth Annual Conference on Taxation* (Columbus: National Tax Association, forthcoming).

5. Although Michigan required the use of a formula apportionment approach, separate accounting was permitted *in lieu* of the formula method if the business received approval from the tax commissioner. Act 150, P. A. 1957, Sec. 205.533 as amended by Act 186, Laws 1965.

base. However, like the separate accounting approach, direct allocation is infrequently used.[6] With this method, a business apportions its tax base by directly allocating certain kinds of items wholly to a single geographical source. For example, capital gains from the sale of real estate are generally allocated to the state in which the property is physically located, income from personal services such as consulting fees is attributed to the state where the service is performed, and interest is allocated to the residence of the lender.[7]

The specific allocation approach has four characteristics which do not recommend its use: (1) the direct allocation of sales is, for practical purposes, impossible in vertically integrated operations; (2) since only certain kinds of expenses are regarded as directly apportionable, the specific allocation method must be used in conjunction with some other apportionment scheme; (3) because particular states treat the same item of income according to different rules, specific allocation leads to a maze of complex compliance problems. A business which has various types of receipts and which is widely taxable cannot determine tax liabilities without familiarity with a broad range of significant and often contradictory rules; and (4) due to the lack of agreement among states in the treatment of various items, multiple taxation or, at the other extreme, no taxation may result.[8]

Formula Apportionment

The most common solution to the problem of apportioning multistate receipts among various state tax jurisdictions is formula apportionment. A business firm computes a ratio which, ostensibly, measures the fraction of its total value or activity applicable to a particular state. The numerator of this ratio measures the amount of business activity or value created within a given state, and the denominator measures total activity or value. The implicit assumption made is that the ultimate source of business income or receipts is located where such value is finally created or where such activity takes place.[9]

---

6. The BAT statute permitted the direct allocation method upon approval of the tax commissioner under paragraph f, Sec. 205.533 C. L., of Act 150, P. A. 153.

7. Beaman, *Paying Taxes to Other States*, pp. 3-5, 3-6.

8. *State Taxation of Interstate Commerce*, vol. 1, p. 216–17.

9. The form of formula apportionment is:

Total Tax Base $\times$ Apportionment Ratio $=$ Apportioned Tax Base, where

The definition of the factors (terms) used in the apportionment ratio varies among the states, and the ratio may be either a one-factor or a multifactor ratio. However, three factors (property, payrolls, and sales) are most often employed.[10]

THE PROPERTY FACTOR. The property factor is generally defined in most states, and specifically in Michigan, as the average value of the real and tangible personal property owned or rented by a business organization and used in a given state during the tax period, divided by the average value of all the taxpayer's real and tangible personal property owned or rented during that period.[11] Property is justified as a tax apportionment factor on the premise that the state government incurs costs because the very existence of property within its borders requires provision of such government inputs or services as police, fire, judicial protection, and the like. Furthermore, it is reasonable to assume that the value of these government inputs is proportional to the value of property serviced or protected. Criticism of the use of the property factor focuses on the method of valuation, when value should be determined, and on the issue of treatment of owner-occupied versus rental property.[12]

THE PAYROLL FACTOR. As is the property factor, the use of a payroll factor, in our case the ratio of Michigan payroll to total payroll of the firm, is justified on the grounds that government acts as a factor of production to business by providing various public goods and services and should be compensated for the cost of these items. That is, since payrolls (wages, salaries, commissions, and any other form of

---

the apportionment ratio equals:

$$\frac{\text{In-state Factor of Measure of Business Activity}}{\text{Total Measure of Business Activity}}$$

Then, to compute the tax due:

Apportioned Tax Base $\times$ Tax Rate $=$ Tax Due.

10. Other factors used by states are manufacturing costs, manufacturing assets, inventory, capital assets, and investment in capital securities. These are listed in *State Taxation of Interstate Commerce*, vol. 1, p. 119.

11. The average value of property was determined by averaging the values at the beginning and ending of a tax period. Property owned by the taxpayer was valued at original cost. Property rented and used by the taxpayer was valued at eight times its annual rental value (the annual rental rate paid by the taxpayer less any annual rental rate received by the taxpayer from subrentals). Act 150, P. A. 1953, Sec. 205.553 and R. 205.566, Rule 16, paragraph 6.

12. For a detailed analysis of these issues, see *State Taxation of Interstate Commerce*, vol. 1, pp. 171–76.

remuneration paid to employees for personal services) are a measure of business activity, and "since that activity is a fair reflection of the state's need for incurring government costs" for such items as "roads, bridges, sidewalks, policemen, airports, hospitals, schools, etc., wherever people live and work," a government recompense may be demanded.[13] There is little criticism of the use of a payroll factor, especially since the data can be simply obtained from business income and unemployment compensation statements.[14]

THE SALES FACTOR. The arithmetic of the sales factor is similar to the property and payroll factors: it is the ratio of sales attributable to the state to total sales receipts. However, the choice of the definition of the numerator of the sales fraction is more complex than is true for property and payrolls. The question arises whether sales should be defined according to origin, that is, the state in which the goods and services are finally produced, or destination, the state in which the goods and services are consumed. The choice is an important one since the size of the sales factor will be affected by the location of the center of economic activity. As a practical matter, the origin principle allocates sales to the state from which the goods are produced and shipped and, as a result, reflects the viewpoint that the tax jurisdiction within which the firm is located provides the government services which permit the firm's production activity. As such, it tends to duplicate the rationale given for the property and payroll factors.[15]

On the other hand, the destination principle is justified on the grounds that it gives recognition to the state actually providing the final marketplace, and is less subject to manipulations for tax avoidance.[16] The major criticism of the destination method is that it not only provides a loophole for local firms which sell outside the state (for example, much of Michigan's durable manufacturing is export orientated), but also fails to recognize the location of the factory or office which actually uses the local government services as a factor of production.

---

13. Beaman, *Paying Taxes to Other States*, p. 3-8.

14. Ratliff, *Interstate Apportionment*, p. 23.

15. There are three major variations in the definition of sales origin: place of manufacture, location of goods, and shipping point. These are discussed in *State Taxation of Interstate Commerce*, vol. 1, p. 187–88. Since 1959, states have been prohibited from taxing business where the only activity is solicitation of orders. *Interstate Income Law*, P. L. 86-272, 73, Stat. 555 (1959).

16. Beaman, *Paying Taxes to Other States*, p. 3-9.

The Michigan BAT statute included sales as one of the three factors in its apportionment formula. The numerator of the sales ratio was defined as gross receipts from the sale of tangible personal property which was delivered or shipped from a factory, store, warehouse, or other place of storage to a purchaser *within* the state regardless of the f.o.b. point or other conditions of sale, plus gross receipts from business other than sales of tangible personal property if all or "a greater proportion" of the income producing activity was within Michigan.[17] Thus the Michigan sales factor definition adopted the destination principle for tangible property, and, less significant, an origin principle for some intangible services.

Choosing the Formula

There is as yet no general agreement either within the national business sector or among state tax administrators regarding the proper apportionment formula to employ. However, several states and many government and legal councils have reacted favorably to a 1957 proposal by the National Conference of Commissioners on Uniform State Laws (NCCUSL) that the three-factor formula, an unweighted average of the sales, property, and payroll factors, be enacted for all states.[18] Nevertheless, there is still no universal agreement on the formula.

One-Factor Formula

The defect of all one-factor apportionment formulas is that they apportion business value activity without considering all factors of

---

17. Act 150, P. A. 1953, Sec. 205.533. The following items serve as a guide for determining Michigan sales. In-state or Michigan sales included: sales to a Michigan customer with shipment being made to a Michigan destination from either a location in Michigan or an out-of-state location; sales to a Michigan customer with shipment being made to a Michigan destination directly from the taxpayer's Michigan supplier or out-of-state supplier; and sales to an out-of-state customer, but with shipment or delivery being made to the customer's location within the state of Michigan. Out-of-state sales included: sales to a Michigan customer with shipments being made directly to the customer at a regularly maintained and established out-of-state place of business for his use at this out-of-state location, and sales to an out-of-state customer with shipment being made to an out-of-state destination.

18. The NCCUSL formula employs the destination criterion for sales, and has been recommended in the Multistate Tax Compact.

production. For example, although the property factor reflects the fact that capital and land resources are important contributors to income and product originating in business, it ignores the contribution of labor. Conversely, a payroll division of the tax base entirely ignores the capital input. A destination sales measure recognizes a different element of business activity than either property or payrolls, namely, that state governments provide the service of the provision of a marketplace for sales activity. However, it ignores the contribution of both labor and property to the production process. Due to weaknesses such as these, one-factor apportionment schemes are rarely used.

Three-Factor Formula

Prior to 1955, the Michigan BAT statute used sales as the only factor for attributing adjusted receipts within and without the state. As a result, the BAT encountered strong criticism for the following reasons: (1) it favored Michigan export industries relative to firms shipping entirely within Michigan; (2) it gave a tax avoidance loophole to firms having out-of-state inventory locations; (3) it led to overtaxation because by taxing 50 percent of interstate receipts as well as all in-state sales, Michigan was essentially taxing on both an origin and a destination basis; and (4) the formula raised questions of constitutionality.[19]

Consequently, the one-factor approach was eliminated in 1955 in favor of multifactor apportionment. In particular, taxpayers generating adjusted receipts were given the option (with approval of the tax commissioner) of either separate accounting methods or the three-factor equal weight (sales, property, payroll) formula. Special ap-

---

19. Lock, Rau, and Hamilton, "The Michigan Value Added Tax," pp. 361–63. The basic formula for computing receipts from Michigan business was the sum of receipts from exclusively Michigan sales, 50 percent of receipts from sales to out-of-state customers, 50 percent of receipts from sales of goods located outside the state but shipped into the state, and 50 percent of receipts from sales of property not located at any permanent or continuous place of business maintained by the taxpayer without the state, such as goods in transit or in warehouses, where the orders were received or accepted within the state. In essence, the tax receipts were those from Michigan sales exclusively plus 50 percent of receipts from interstate transactions. Commerce Clearing House, *New Michigan Business Receipts Tax* (Chicago: Commerce Clearing House, 1953), para. 98-023–32.

portionment formulas were included for various types of transportation activities.

Two-Factor Formula

Although the unweighted three-factor approach is now employed by a majority of apportioning states,[20] recent attention has been given to both an unweighted and a weighted two-factor payroll and property formula. The advocates of the unweighted formula argue that all business income (for example, net income, adjusted receipts, gross receipts) arises from the input of property and labor and, furthermore, that the elimination of the sales factor is justified on conceptual as well as on practical grounds of taxpayer compliance. Indeed, if interstate firms were to pay income type taxes in all states in which they make sales, most businesses would be subject to so many tax forms and obligations that they would be unable to cope with compliance requirements.[21]

Proponents of a weighted two-factor formula also criticize the inclusion of a sales element in the multistate apportionment formula, but further point out that since the two-factor approach is designed to reflect all income and production, the labor–capital mix in the production function also should be considered. Thus it would be necessary to give the payroll factor from two to four times the weight of the property factor.[22] Although the proposal for the weighting of the payroll factor is theoretically sound, there is a practical obstacle involved since there are variations among industries regarding the actual proportion of labor and capital in the production process.

In order to illustrate how a Michigan firm would apply these various apportionment formulas, consider the following hypothetical example. Assume a firm with multistate operations has total adjusted

---

20. Advisory Commission on Intergovernmental Relations, *State and Local Finances: Significant Features 1967 to 1970,* Report M-50 (Washington, D.C.: U.S. Government Printing Office, 1969), p. 180.

21. For example, see C. Lowell Harris, "Income Apportionment Among the States: A Sales Factor Does Not Belong in the Formula," in *Seminar on the Taxation of Interstate Business* (New York: Tax Foundation, Inc., 1970), pp. 63–68.

22. Beaman, *Paying Taxes to Other States,* p. 3–15. For purposes in the study, payroll was given three times the weight of property:

$$\frac{3 \times (\text{Payroll Ratio}) + \text{Property Ratio}}{\text{Sum of Weights}}$$

receipts of $8,000,000, an in-state (Michigan) payroll of $1,500,000, property worth $20,000,000, and sales of $5,000,000. Total payroll, property, and sales equal $4,500,000, $8,000,000, and $50,000,000 respectively. The allocation ratio to be applied to the $8,000,000 tax base are:

For sales only (destination):

$$\frac{\text{Michigan sales}}{\text{Total sales}} = \frac{\$5,000,000}{\$50,000,000} = 10.0\%;$$

for the equal weight three-factor ratio:

$$\frac{\dfrac{\text{Michigan sales}}{\text{Total sales}} + \dfrac{\text{Michigan property}}{\text{Total property}} + \dfrac{\text{Michigan payroll}}{\text{Total payroll}}}{3}$$

$$= \frac{\dfrac{\$5,000,000}{\$50,000,000} + \dfrac{\$20,000,000}{\$80,000,000} + \dfrac{\$1,500,000}{\$4,500,000}}{3}$$

$$= \frac{.10 + .25 + .33}{3} = 22.7\% .$$

Similarly, for the equal weight two-factor ratio:

$$\frac{\dfrac{\text{Michigan property}}{\text{Total property}} + \dfrac{\text{Michigan payroll}}{\text{Total payroll}}}{2} = 29.0\% ;$$

for the weighted two-factor ratio:

$$\frac{\dfrac{\text{Michigan property}}{\text{Total property}} + 3 \dfrac{\text{Michigan payroll}}{\text{Total payroll}}}{4} = 33.5\%.$$

In this example, the weighted average approach yields the largest tax to Michigan because the firm's activity is one which employed a greater percentage of its total labor than of its total property in the Michigan production process. The sales destination factor, however, yields the smallest tax base to Michigan since the hypothetical firm is export orientated. Similarly, the sales factor dampens the three-factor apportionment formula relative to both of the two-factor approaches.

This example illustrates the tax base division relationships only; without prior statements regarding both the government revenue goals and the structure of the in-state business sector, it gives little guide as to which of the above formulas a state may prefer to adopt. That is, if a state is, like Michigan, export orientated, then from a revenue productivity viewpoint the sales and the three-factor formulas would be the least desirable apportionment ratios. However, for a state which is a net goods importer, clearly the inclusion of the sales factor would increase revenues.[23]

Multistate Adjusted Receipts

Data from actual 1965 BAT returns were analyzed in order to provide empirical estimates of the relative tax liability effects of the alternative apportionment formulas on Michigan industry.[24] Computations were made for the following ratios: sales only (destination); equal weight property and payroll; sales (destination), property, and payrolls; and weighted payrolls and property: 3 × (Payroll) + Property. Table 26 presents the percentage change of major industry BAT liabilities under the four formulas. The three-factor approach which was actually used in Michigan is the base measure.

If Michigan had adopted the sales factor approach, the mining and manufacturing sectors would have experienced a large relative decrease in their tax liabilities, enough of a decline, in fact, to cause the entire Michigan BAT collections to decline by more than one-third from the sales-property-payroll approach levels. Conversely, a switch to either of the two-factor approaches not only would have increased the tax obligations of mining and manufacturing, but also would have had a positive effect on total revenue, increasing collections by 18.5 percent under the weighted scheme, and by 17.8 percent under the equal weight approach.[25]

---

23. Of course, such motives of fiscal mercantilism are not limited to governments. The adoption of a sales only factor in the original BAT statute is not surprising once one considers that the large manufacturing tangible goods export industries, in particular motor vehicle industry representatives, were the main architects of the original act.

24. See Appendix C for description of the empirical work.

25. In 1965 legislation was introduced into the U.S. House of Representatives which implemented a recommendation of the Special Subcommittee on State Taxation (see footnote 4) that states be required to employ an unweighted two-factor formula (property and payroll) for apportioning interstate receipts. H.R. 11798, U.S. House of Representatives, 89th Cong., 1st sess.

TABLE 26. Percentage Relationships of BAT Liabilities, Various Apportionment Formulas for Multistate Adjusted Receipts, by Industry, Firms with Tax Due Greater than $5,000, 1965

Industry	Sales only		Payroll and property		Sales, payroll, and property		Weighted payroll and property	
	Percentage[a]	*Index*[b]	*Percentage*[a]	*Index*[b]	*Percentage*[a]	*Index*[b]	*Percentage*[a]	*Index*[b]
Mining	−32.4	76.6	16.2	116.2	0.0	100.0	13.2	113.2
Construction	−.3	99.7	.4	100.4	0.0	100.0	−.3	99.7
Manufacturing	−55.9	44.1	28.1	128.1	0.0	100.0	29.3	129.3
Utilities	1.8	101.8	−.9	99.1	0.0	100.0	−.8	99.2
Wholesale trade	25.9	125.9	−12.1	87.9	0.0	100.0	−13.7	86.3
Retail trade	3.0	103.0	−1.5	98.5	0.0	100.0	.9	100.9
Services	2.4	102.4	−1.4	98.6	0.0	100.0	−.8	99.2
All industry	−35.3	64.7	17.8	117.8	0.0	100.0	18.5	118.5

SOURCE: Business Activities Tax returns supplied by Michigan Department of Treasury, Revenue Division.
[a] Change relative to three-factor formula.
[b] Three-factor formula equals 100.0.

The actual dollar tax payments and each major industry's percentage of the total BAT obligation are presented in Table 27. From an examination of these data it is clear that, relative to the three-factor approach employed in 1965, tax costs would have decreased for mining, construction, and manufacturing (especially the durable goods industry) under the sales factor ratio method, and that only mining and manufacturing tax costs would have increased due to adoption of either of the two-factor apportionment fractions. In addition, the table provides information to support the statement that Michigan manufacturing is a large goods exporter, as is mining. Also, the importance of the payroll–property mix in the Michigan production process of various industries can be determined. A comparison of figures in the two property–payroll factor columns indicates that in-state payroll was more important in percentage terms in the production function than was in-state property for the mining, manufacturing, utility, retail trade, and service industries.

Because of the importance of manufacturing in the Michigan business sector generally (manufacturing accounted for 47 percent of total gross state production in 1965), and specifically due to the obvious effect on the direction of total BAT liabilities of the manufacturing sector, a further breakdown of manufacturing is warranted. These data are provided in Tables 28 and 29.

Table 28 presents percentage relationships of tax liabilities for the alternative formulas (again with the sales-property-payroll factor as the base), by type of manufacturer, for firms with tax due of $5,000 or more. In general, most manufacturers would experience increased tax liabilities under either two-factor proposals and decreased tax obligations using a sales only approach. As is indicated in Table 29, which shows tax collection data for taxpayers by type of manufacturers, the revenue loss to Michigan as a result of the use of a sales destination factor is particularly significant in the case of the transportation equipment sector. For example, exclusive use of the sales factor would have reduced their tax obligations by nearly 74 percent. Table 29 data, therefore, not only give an historical perspective regarding the revenue effect of the original BAT apportionment scheme, but also indicate

(1965). Subsequently, other legislation has been introduced into both the U.S. House and Senate which prescribes this two-factor approach on an optional basis. For example, H.R. 7906, U.S. House of Representatives, 91st Cong., 1st sess. (1969); and S. Z17, U.S. Senate, 92nd Cong., 1st sess. (1971), esp. sec. 201-203.

TABLE 27.   BAT Payments, Various Apportionment Formulas for Multistate Adjusted Receipts, by Industry, Firms with Tax Due Greater than $5,000, 1965

Industry	Sales only		Payroll and property		Sales, payroll, and property		Weighted payroll and property	
	Thousands of dollars	Percentage composition	Thousands of dollars	Percentage composition	Thousands of dollars	Percentage composition	Thousands of dollars	Percentage composition
Agriculture	(NA)*	(NA)	(NA)	(NA)	1,595	1.6	(NA)	(NA)
Mining	435	0.7	719	0.6	644	0.6	729	0.6
Construction	5,078	7.9	5,114	4.4	5,094	5.0	5,078	4.4
Manufacturing	27,766	43.0	80,653	70.0	62,961	63.0	81,409	70.1
Nondurables	6,019	9.4	17,744	15.4	13,851	13.9	17,910	15.4
Durables	21,657	33.6	62,909	54.6	49,110	49.1	63,499	54.7
Utilities	8,106	12.6	7,891	6.9	7,936	7.9	7,899	6.8
Wholesale trade	5,220	8.1	3,668	3.2	4,173	4.2	3,601	3.1
Retail trade	8,759	13.6	8,376	7.3	8,504	8.5	8,581	7.4
Services	9,098	14.1	8,761	7.6	8,885	8.9	8,814	7.6
Other	(NA)	(NA)	(NA)	(NA)	96	0.2	(NA)	(NA)
All industry	64,462	100.0	115,182	100.0	99,888	100.0	116,111	100.0

SOURCES: Computed from Table 11, column 3, and Table 26. Data supplied by Michigan Department of Treasury, Revenue Division.

*Not available. See Appendix C.

TABLE 28. Percentage Relationships of BAT Liabilities, Various Apportionment Formulas for Multistate Adjusted Receipts, by Manufacturer, Firms with Tax Due Greater than $5,000, 1965

Manufacturer	Sales only		Payroll and property		Sales, payroll, and property		Weighted payroll and property	
	Percentage[a]	Index[b]	Percentage[a]	Index[b]	Percentage[a]	Index[b]	Percentage[a]	Index[b]
Food and kindred products	−32.5	67.5	15.6	115.6	0.0	100.0	16.7	116.7
Furniture and fixtures	−21.9	78.1	11.5	111.5	0.0	100.0	11.7	111.7
Printing and publishing	−38.9	61.1	19.4	119.4	0.0	100.0	18.2	118.2
Chemicals and allied products	.1	100.1	8.4	108.4	0.0	100.0	12.2	112.2
Stone, clay, and glass	25.1	125.1	−12.0	88.0	0.0	100.0	−10.6	89.4
Primary metal	47.4	147.4	−24.8	75.2	0.0	100.0	−19.2	80.8
Fabricated metal	−19.9	80.1	8.6	108.6	0.0	100.0	8.5	108.5
Machinery, except electrical	−25.6	74.4	13.3	113.3	0.0	100.0	17.4	117.4
Electrical machinery	25.4	125.4	−14.4	85.6	0.0	100.0	−11.5	88.5
Transportation equipment	−72.3	27.7	36.0	136.0	0.0	100.0	36.7	136.7
Total nondurable products	−15.7	84.3	11.9	111.9	0.0	100.0	14.1	114.1
Total durable products	−59.2	40.8	29.5	129.5	0.0	100.0	30.6	130.6
Total	−55.9	44.1	28.1	128.1	0.0	100.0	29.3	129.3

SOURCE: Business Activities Tax returns supplied by Michigan Department of Treasury, Revenue Division.
[a] Change relative to three-factor formula.
[b] Three-factor formula equals 100.0.

TABLE 29. **Percentage Relationships of BAT Liabilities, Various Apportionment Formulas for Multistate Adjusted Receipts, by Manufacturer, Firms with Tax Due Greater than $50,000, 1965**

Manufacturer[a]	*Sales only*		*Payroll and property*		*Sales, payroll, and property*		*Weighted payroll and property*	
	Percentage[b]	*Index*[c]	*Percentage*[b]	*Index*[c]	*Percentage*[b]	*Index*[c]	*Percentage*[b]	*Index*[c]
Food and kindred products	-45.7	54.3	21.6	121.6	0.0	100.0	23.6	123.6
Furniture and fixtures	-12.8	87.2	7.0	107.0	0.0	100.0	6.5	106.5
Chemicals and allied products	-9.0	91.0	14.6	114.6	0.0	100.0	19.2	119.2
Primary metal	59.0	159.0	-30.8	69.2	0.0	100.0	-26.3	73.7
Fabricated metal	-19.0	81.0	8.8	108.8	0.0	100.0	8.3	108.3
Machinery, except electrical	-35.1	64.9	17.1	117.1	0.0	100.0	23.8	123.8
Electrical machinery	31.4	131.4	-17.7	82.3	0.0	100.0	-14.9	85.1
Transportation equipment	-73.7	26.3	36.8	136.8	0.0	100.0	37.4	137.4
Total	-61.0	39.0	30.6	130.6	0.0	100.0	31.7	131.7

SOURCE: Computed from tax return data supplied by Michigan Department of Treasury, Revenue Division.
[a]Some manufacturing groups not included due to poor data.
[b]Change relative to three-factor formula.
[c]Three-factor formula equals 100.0.

the relative effect on revenue productivity due to the inclusion of sales destination in the conventional three-factor approach. Tables 28 and 29 also indicate that transportation equipment, nonelectrical machinery, and food products industries are all large exporters. On the other hand, the primary metals and electrical machine manufacturers are large goods suppliers to Michigan.

In conclusion, it is important to reiterate that the Michigan data are of value not only in order to understand the Michigan BAT and the state industry effects, but also because the issue of alternative multistate tax base apportionment formulas is currently under congressional consideration. Furthermore, although these empirical results are based on Michigan — a heavy manufacturing orientated state — these data (with some modification) could serve as a guide to the effects the various apportionment formulas would have in other large manufacturing states.[26]

---

26. These results do not necessarily contradict the conclusion of the study by the House Committee on the Judiciary that in choosing among alternative formulas revenue considerations are minor. As the House study points out, due to the importance of its manufacturing sector Michigan is the extreme case in such revenue tests. See *State Taxation of Interstate Commerce*, vol. 1, chap. 16, esp. pp. 531, 561–62.

9

Economic and Administrative Aspects of Selected Provisions

Rationale for Taxation

Throughout this study it has been implicitly assumed that there exists an acceptable rationale for taxing business enterprise. Before making an appraisal of some of the major statutory features of the BAT, it is now appropriate to examine this assumption. Such an analysis will provide a normative framework for subsequent discussion of the economic effects of the BAT, preparatory to addressing the question of whether, in the light of the arguments commonly presented to justify various types of business taxes, the BAT can be reasonably rationalized as a form of state business taxation. The importance of this discussion of rationale is not limited to the specific question of the BAT. It has implications for measuring structural industry tax inequality (see pages 72–79) as well as for applying a particular apportionment formula to interstate business receipts (see pages 103–107).

Justifications for Broad-Based Taxation

The role of the business enterprise in the flow of economic activity is one of organizing production and creating income. That is, the business firm is the institution through which individuals, in their roles as consumers or owners (suppliers) of factors of production, derive the benefits of economic activity. As a result of this organizational function, business institutions become a convenient, efficient, and expedient instrument for collecting taxes.[1] This practical justification, however, cannot override the elementary fact that ultimately all taxes are paid by individuals, not by business or, for that matter, by entities such as real estate, capital stock, or gasoline. A tax levied on business is paid by its customers (in higher prices), resource suppliers (in lower wages to labor or lower profits for entrepreneurs), and owners (in reduction of equity).[2] As will all taxes, business taxes ultimately will reduce the individual's income or equity available for disposal in the private economy.

Given this principle, the question arises of whether there is justification, other than fiscal expediency, for taxing business, that is, for taxing income at its source rather than at the place of personal receipt or disposition. The answer will depend on the characteristics of the institutional structure of the economy. In the closed economy, an economy isolated from the rest of the world, there is little, if any, need to use source taxation; the objectives of budget policy regarding revenue productivity, resource allocation, and distribution of the tax burden can best be achieved through direct personal taxation.[3] Although no economy, of course, is completely closed, a national economy, which has the authority to restrict extra-tax jurisdictional activities through various nonmarket imposed economic barriers, does approximate this structure. The closer this approximation, the less justification there is for a recourse to general business taxation.[4]

---

1. Colm has labeled this rationalization for taxing business as the "cynical rule of fiscal productivity." Studenski describes this same concept as the "social expediency theory of business taxation." See Gerhard Colm, "Conflicting Theories of Corporate Income Taxation," *Law and Contemporary Problems* 7 (Spring 1940): 282; and Paul Studenski, "Toward a Theory of Business Taxation," *Journal of Political Economy* 68 (October 1940): 639–40.

2. A business's customer, of course, may be another business. Eventually, however, the tax will be paid out of the individual's income or equity.

3. Because general business taxation is indirect in that it involves further market transactions, many additional economic and institutional factors tend to disguise the ultimate effects of taxes on people, and make achievement of these tax policy goals more difficult.

4. National economies vary in their degrees of closeness. At one extreme are such countries as Venezuela and Burma, which have net exports as high

Unlike a national economy, tax jurisdictions operating in open economies lack the authority to place artificial restrictions on labor, capital, and commodity mobility across their borders (for example, tariffs, quotas, various legal and administrative trade regulations, immigration laws, and the like).[5] One obvious implication of this openness is that nonresident individuals owning all or part of a resident business enterprise cannot be taxed directly on their income, wealth, or wealth transfers.[6] Similarly, resident individuals can engage in spending beyond the jurisdictional authority of the resident state, including purchases of goods produced within the state of residence and, therefore, can avoid direct payments under conventional sales and consumption taxes. A somewhat different, although related, budgetary implication of this economic openness is that externality benefits resulting from subnational government expenditure programs affect individuals beyond the borders of the taxing jurisdiction. For example, state of Michigan services to automobile producers indirectly benefit factory workers commuting from Ohio, or motorists in Oregon.

For the foregoing reasons, a crucial tax policy difference exists between national and subnational jurisdictions.[7] Operating in essentially closed economies, national governments do not need to be concerned with factor and goods mobility or with the externality benefits of public services. Thus, other than for reasons of expediency, no recourse to source (in this case business) taxation is required. For open subnational governments, however, the taxation of business becomes

---

as one-third to one-half of their national income. At the other extreme are countries such as the United States, the exports of which usually are less than 6 percent of national income. Sources: Delbert A. Snider, *International Economics* (Homewood, Ill.: Richard D. Irwin, Inc., 1967), p. 12; and U.S. Department of Commerce, Office of Business Economics, *Survey of Current Business* (Washington, D.C.: U.S. Government Printing Office, July 1970), Table A-1, p. 14.

5. In 1962 the total value of Michigan's agricultural, mining, and manufacturing shipments was $27,880,875. Of this amount, $21,423,361, or 76.8 percent of total shipment, was shipped out of state. Source: John L. Hazard, *Michigan Commerce: Domestic and International*, Technical Report No. 5 (Lansing: Michigan Department of Commerce, 1966), Exhibit VII, p. 28.

6. Much of the discussion of the asymmetry between tax policy for open and closed economies is from Robert D. Ebel and James A. Papke, "A Closer Look at the Value Added Tax," pp. 157–59.

7. Other differences such as those related to the objectives of income distribution and stabilization policies are not directly relevant to this topic and are not discussed here.

the only source available for assessing individual customers, factor owners, and wealth holders, wherever they may reside, for the services which initially accrue to business entities.

Choosing the Tax Base

The case to justify taxation of business within the open economy context does not present any *a priori* argument regarding the proper base for business taxation. The next step is to establish criteria for choosing that base. The topic has been the subject of many professional discussions, and no attempt will be made here to reiterate these general theories and to discuss their various merits and defects.[8] Rather, attention will be directed toward the conceptual issue of the choice of the tax base as applied to the Michigan experience. In particular, in the context of the BAT, the most commonly employed concepts for choosing a base, ability to pay and benefits received, were constantly at odds with one another. In policy studies and councils these two concepts were represented by the practical choice between business net income or the value-added type tax base (adjusted receipts).[9]

THE NET INCOME BASE. A rationale used to justify general taxation of business, particularly on a net income basis, is the impersonal ability concept, namely, that with a tax levied on net income "the success that gives rise to the tax liability also produces means for its payment."[10] The implication of this viewpoint is that business firms have, as separate entities, a taxpaying capacity that can be distinguished

---

8. See, for example, Thomas S. Adams, "The Taxation of Business," in *Proceedings of the Eleventh Annual Conference on Taxation* (New York: National Tax Association, 1917), p. 185 ff.; Harvey D. Brazer, "The Value of Industrial Property as a Subject of Taxation," *Journal of Canadian Public Administration* 4 (March 1961): 137–42; Colm, "Conflicting Theories," p. 281 ff.; Richard Goode, *The Corporation Income Tax* (New York: John Wiley and Sons, Inc., 1951), pp. 24–43; Papke, "The Taxation of Business Enterprise," pp. 559–69; Studenski, "Toward a Theory," p. 621 ff.; and Tax Institute, *Reappraisal of Business Taxation,* a Symposium Conducted by the Tax Institute of America, Inc. (Princeton: Princeton University Press, 1962), p. 242.

9. Just as a conceptual justification for taxing business does not define the type of tax base, neither does the acceptance of a theory of business taxation establish a given proper basis for the levy. However, because the so-called ability and benefits theorists defended the net income and adjusted receipts bases respectively, the discussion in this study reflects that approach.

10. See *Taxes and Economic Growth,* p. 11.

from individuals as stockholders, customers, or employers. The logical conclusion of this argument is that the tax base should be business net income. Just as profits determine the extent to which a business can add to its capital, grant wage increases, and improve working conditions, so do they measure the extent to which the enterprise is able to sustain taxation. In short, state business taxation is viewed as an extension of ability to pay as it is applied to individuals.[11]

THE BROADER ADJUSTED RECEIPTS BASE. The basic argument used to justify the broad-based nature of the BAT was that a state provides various types of services which benefit business firms, and that the firm should pay for these government services which, fundamentally, function as a fifth factor of production. Businesses should pay tax costs for government-provided inputs just as they pay for private inputs of labor (wages), land (rent), capital (interest), and entrepreneurship (profits).

The firm's value added is considered a reasonable business tax base measure by proponents of this benefits concept of taxation for three reasons. (1) Value added represents the total income generated by a firm — the one base which applies to all incomes arising within the tax jurisdiction (a direct link to the open versus closed economy discussion, a link profits taxation proponents cannot make).[12] (2) Value added measures the total value of private inputs used by the firm and, therefore, serves as a proximate measure to differentiate the value of actual government services provided to different firms. That is, from a resource market view, value added measures the extent to which business employs society's economic resources, namely, land, labor, capital, and entrepreneurial skills. Thus, a flat rate tax levied on value added measures society's relative contribution to the firm's activity — the larger a firm's employment of society's scarce resources, the greater the social (tax) charge for that use. In essence, this social (government) factor is assumed proportional to the firm's employment of private sector resources, where the government input is viewed in a broader context than only the provision of particular services such as

---

11. Studenski, "Toward a Theory," pp. 633–34, and 634n. A recent Tax Foundation report discusses the point that the conventional wisdom today is that business has a separate taxpaying capacity. See Committee on Federal Tax Policy, *Taxing Business Enterprise: Some Principles* (New York: Tax Foundation, Inc., 1969), p. 31.

12. The logical conclusion here is that the value-added tax should yield revenue to cover the cost of exported services.

police or fire protection.[13] (3) A value-added measure extends the tax obligation to all businesses which receive government services, regardless of the type of legal organization or level of profitability.

These arguments can be extended to justify the nature of the BAT on the basis that the BAT and a pure value-added tax were the same in principle: they both emphasized the view that the business enterprise is the originator of income and wealth. The difference between a value-added levy and the BAT was due to structure and not to rationale.

Equalization of the Tax Base

Once the justification for state business taxation has been established and the firm's adjusted receipts have been accepted as the measure of the tax base, then it follows that for various business taxpayers the size of the tax base and (given a flat statutory rate) the tax contribution will not be uniform. Tax liability will be a function of variations in the proportion of itemized deductions (interfirm purchases) to gross receipts. In general, the computation of the BAT liability was consistent with this concept. However, there were three major statutory provisions which conceptually violated the premise that adjusted receipts were the index of tax base equality among taxpayers. These were the minimum deduction, the excess payroll deduction, and the specific dollar exemption.

The minimum deduction provision, which permitted the taxpayer to take a standard deduction of 50 percent of total gross receipts *in lieu* of itemizing, reduced the absolute and relative tax obligation of firms which had a low ratio of interfirm purchases to gross receipts. Furthermore, in the cases of firms using this optional minimum deduction in combination with the specific dollar exemption, the result could have been a decrease in the number of taxpayers reporting and a reduction in the tax base against which rates were applied. For example, an average service trade firm had allowable itemized deductions equal to 31.4 percent of gross receipts.[14] Given the $12,-500 specific dollar exemption, dollar amounts of gross receipts above $18,222 theoretically were taxable. However, by electing to use the

---

13. This view taken to its logical conclusion dictates that the firm's value-added base includes the dollar outlay to private factors as well as to the government factor for the direct cost of public goods and services.

14. See Table 30, column 1.

standard deduction, the minimum taxable gross receipts would be $25,000. Thus, firms with gross receipts greater than $18,222, but less than $25,000, were excluded from the tax.[15]

The attempt to equalize (in fact, minimize) tax payments was furthered by the supplementary payroll deduction, which permitted a firm to take total deductions equal to a maximum of 60 percent of gross receipts, and by the specific dollar exemption of the first $12,500 of a taxpayer's adjusted receipts base. The principal objective of the $12,500 specific dollar exemption was to relieve small business enterprises from the tax, and thereby avoid the administrative cost of collecting from taxpayers whose tax payments would not justify the expense, but the provision was extended to large and small firms alike. The elimination of this provision for the 109,557 taxpayers reporting in 1965 would have increased the total BAT tax collections by $4,494,-964 — more than 4.5 percent. On the other hand, there was no major taxpayer group which, as an industry, qualified for the supplementary payroll deduction.[16]

Comprehensiveness

In order to determine the *de facto* coverage of the BAT, measures of the practical effect of the combination of allowable deductions and the specific dollar exemption were computed for major industry groups and by manufacturing industry.[17] Minimum gross tax data are presented in Tables 30 and 31 for major industry groups and for manu-

---

15. According to Rule 1 of Michigan Department of Treasury, Revenue Division, *Business Activities Tax Rules and Regulation* (1967), no return was required from any person having gross receipts of less than $25,000 during his fiscal year.

16. Estimates were made from taxpayer data in *Annual Report*, 1965, and tax base information in chapter 4 and Tables 1 and A-1 in *An Econometric Model of Michigan*.

17. Estimates of the minimum gross receipts taxed by industry type were computed as follows:

Let GR = Minimum Gross taxed, and
    TAD = Total Allowable Deductions (itemized).

Find: $GR - [TAD + \$12,500] = 0$,
    that is, find that value of GR such that value less total allowable deductions and the specific dollar exemption gives a tax base equal to zero.

facturing groups respectively. The first column in each of these tables presents the ratio of total itemized allowable deductions from the taxpayer's gross receipts permitted in the BAT statute. The next two columns indicate the minimum dollar amount of gross receipts that a representative firm must have in order to be subject to a tax obligation under, first, the $10,000 and, second, the $12,500 specific dollar exemption.[18]

The data in Table 30 indicate that, on the average, only agriculture and services had a ratio of itemized deductions to gross receipts of less than 50 percent, and thus would have used the optional minimum deduction provision.[19] There are, however, other industries which had an average itemized deduction–gross receipts ratio near the 50 percent level and probably would have had a large number of taxpayers benefiting from the minimum deduction provision. Mining, construction, and utilities fall into this group for the major classifications, and nonelectrical machinery is in this range within manufacturing.

The extent of the coverage of the BAT as a general business levy is further indicated from the data presented in Table 32. This table provides estimates of the percentage of firms in each major industry exempted from the BAT, and the percentage of each industry's total gross receipts attributable to the exempted firms. The data are based on the minimum gross tax levels presented in Table 30. Three points of information regarding the pattern and comprehensiveness of the BAT can be derived from an examination of Table 32. First, it is evident from a comparison of the data for all industrial groups that unincorporated business, relative to total (corporate and noncorporate)

Therefore, $GR - [\beta\ (GR) + \$12,500] = 0$,
where β = percentage of total allowable deduction to gross receipts.

Then: $GR\ (1 - \beta) = \$12,500$, or
$$GR = \frac{(\$12,500)}{(1 - \beta)}$$

Note: $\beta = 0.5$ is the minimum deduction; if $\beta > 0.5$ the firm elects to itemize.

18. Prior to 1960 the specific dollar exemption was $10,000.

19. In particular, the personal services (for example, laundry services, beauty and barber shops) classification within the service trade group had an average deduction to gross receipts ratio of less than 30 percent, and would have benefited from the provision.

TABLE 30. Average Allowable BAT Deductions and Minimum Gross Receipts Taxed, by Industry, 1965

Industry	Average deduction: itemized deductions as percentage of gross receipts	Minimum gross receipts taxed at $10,000 specific exemption (in dollars)	Minimum gross receipts taxed at $12,500 specific exemption (in dollars)
Agriculture	—[a]	20,000	25,000
Mining	52.1	20,877	26,096
Construction	51.7	20,704	25,880
Manufacturing	59.1	24,450	30,526
Utilities	53.0	21,322	26,652
Wholesale trade	85.0	66,667	83,333
Retail trade	67.0	30,303	37,879
Services	31.4	20,000	25,000
All industry	56.2[b]	22,831	28,539

SOURCES: Computed from tax returns supplied by the Michigan Department of Treasury, Revenue Division; U.S. Department of Treasury, Internal Revenue Service, *Statistics of Income: Business Income Tax Returns* (Washington, D.C.: Government Printing Office, 1965); Daniel B. Suits, *Econometric Model of Michigan*, Technical Report No. 3 (Lansing: Michigan Department of Commerce, 1966); and Harvey E. Brazer et al., *General Fund Estimates of Revenue and Expenditures to 1975*, Technical Report No. 11 (Lansing: Michigan Department of Commerce, 1967).

[a]Due to poor data for agriculture, exact estimates were not computed. However, secondary national sources clearly indicate that agriculture would have used the minimum standard deduction.

[b]Unweighted average.

TABLE 31. Average Allowable BAT Deductions and Minimum Gross Receipts Taxed, by Manufacturer, 1965

Manufacturer	Average deduction: itemized deductions as percentage of gross receipts	Minimum gross receipts taxed at $10,000 specific exemption (in dollars)	Minimum gross receipts taxed at $12,500 specific exemption (in dollars)
Food and kindred products	72.7	36,360	47,788
Furniture and fixtures	59.5	24,691	30,864
Paper and allied products	54.1	20,202	25,253
Printing and publishing	54.3	21,882	27,352
Chemicals and allied products	58.1	23,866	29,833
Rubber and plastics	64.1	27,855	34,819
Stone, clay, and glass	57.1	23,641	29,551
Primary metal	59.2	24,510	30,637
Fabricated metal	66.2	29,586	36,982
Machinery, except electrical	51.9	20,790	25,988
Electrical machinery	58.3	23,981	29,976
Transportation equipment	56.9	23,202	29,002
Total	59.1	24,450	30,562

SOURCES: Computed from tax returns supplied by the Michigan Department of Treasury, Revenue Division; U.S. Department of Treasury, Internal Revenue Service, Statistics of Income: Business Income Tax Returns (Washington, D.C.: Government Printing Office, 1965); Daniel B. Suits, Econometric Model of Michigan, Technical Report No. 3 (Lansing: Michigan Department of Commerce, 1966); Harvey E. Brazer et al., General Fund Estimates of Revenue and Expenditures to 1975, Technical Report No. 11 (Lansing: Michigan Department of Commerce, 1967); and U.S. Department of Commerce, Bureau of Census, Annual Survey of Manufacturers, 1965 (Washington, D.C.: Government Printing Office, 1968), pp. 243–45.

business, had a greater dollar amount of its gross receipts excluded from the scope of the BAT. To illustrate, sole proprietorships and partnerships respectively had 24.1 and 4.5 percent of their gross receipts below the minimum level of gross receipts taxed by the Michigan BAT. In contrast, only 3.8 percent of total business gross receipts was below this minimum tax level. Similar illustrations could be made with reference to each of the eight major industry groups.

Second, the practical importance of the deductions–specific dollar exemption combination can be shown for each of the industry classifications relative to the other industry groups. For example, it is clear that the agriculture and service trade categories had the largest relative amount of gross receipts excluded from the BAT tax base compared to other industry types. Conversely, nearly all manufacturing receipts were included in the *de facto* scope of the BAT. This latter fact is due particularly to the influence of corporate manufacturing, which had more than 99 percent of all its gross receipts subject to the BAT levy.

Third, the relative concentration of business receipts within separate industry groups is seen by comparing the percentage of firms exempted from the BAT to the percentage of the value of the receipts of these firms which were excluded from the BAT base due to minimum gross tax levels. Wholesale trade is a good example. Nearly 80 percent of wholesale trade sole proprietorship establishments were excluded from the BAT base, but these firms accounted for less than 19 percent of the total gross receipts generated by this industry group. Similarly, the 37.4 percent of corporate wholesale establishments which were excluded from the tax base represented less than 1 percent of the total receipts of all corporate wholesalers. For the total wholesale industry, although almost two-thirds of the establishments were excluded from the BAT's coverage, 97.6 percent of the total dollar value of receipts from wholesalers was taxable.

The data in Tables 30 through 32 are consistent with the hypothesis that the BAT structural tax impact pattern (chapter 7) resulted from the practical effect of the combination of the various deduction provisions and the specific dollar exemption. Although the BAT statute did exclude a large percentage of the total number of business establishments from the tax levy in terms of the total dollar value of receipts generated, the BAT was quite comprehensive. This not only suggests that the tax was, indeed, a general business levy in terms of business activity, but also indicates that, for practical administration and compliance purposes, the BAT eliminated a large

TABLE 32. Percentage of Total Firms and BAT Minimum Levels, by Industry and Type of Business, 1965

Industry	Proprietorships Percentage of total below minimum gross receipts level		Partnerships Percentage of total below minimum gross receipts level		Corporations Percentage of total below minimum gross receipts level		Total business Percentage of total below minimum gross receipts level	
	Number of firms	Gross receipts	Number of firms	Gross receipts	Number of firms	Gross receipts	Number of firms	Gross receipts
Agriculture	87.4	47.1	53.7	11.6	20.4	0.8	85.8	35.5
Mining	63.1	15.8	59.5	5.1	19.0	0.2	57.6	1.6
Construction	23.3	18.5	35.9	3.0	8.1	0.2	22.8	4.4
Manufacturing	65.1	15.0	36.5	2.7	6.1	—a	39.8	0.3
Utilities	84.2	33.7	47.1	6.4	21.0	0.2	75.6	2.2
Wholesale trade	79.6	18.9	39.3	2.9	37.4	0.6	65.9	2.4
Retail trade	58.2	12.5	34.5	4.0	6.4	0.3	50.1	3.8
Services	82.4	33.9	44.1	5.4	23.3	1.5	77.4	14.0
All industry[b]	75.6	24.1	43.8	4.5	12.4	0.2	69.2	3.8

Sources: U.S. Department of Treasury, Internal Revenue Service, *Statistics of Income: Business Income Tax Returns* (Washington, D.C.: Government Printing Office, 1968), Tables 2.2, 3.3, and 5.4; and Michigan data, Table 30.
aLess than 0.1 percent.
bWeighted average.

number of taxpayers (nearly 70 percent of all firms), but at a relatively small revenue loss (3.8 percent).

Administration and Compliance

The business firm's BAT obligation was payable in quarterly installments,[20] the first three of which required the business to make reasonable estimates of only four items: gross receipts, total deductions, taxable balance (gross receipts less deductions for cost of merchandise sold or 50 percent of gross receipts, and one-fourth of the specific dollar exemption), and the tax due. At the end of the taxpayer's fiscal year, the firm filed the annual return. In computing the tax liability, the firm's compliance effort was minimized because all data required for the return could be obtained either from its income statement or from its federal income tax form.

Although the BAT statute eliminated many small taxpayers from the scope of the tax, approximately 96 percent of the total value of business receipts generated in Michigan were covered. The elimination of small establishments from a business tax base has two positive effects. First, it lowers administrative costs by eliminating a large number of taxpayers least familiar with the mechanics of the return, thus requiring government assistance to compute tax liability, and by reducing the total number of returns filed.[21] Second, by eliminating the small taxpayer, total business taxpayer compliance costs also are reduced.[22]

Both administrators and business executives agreed that because the BAT required a minimum of records and was simple to compute it met the objectives of certainty and simplicity in government ad-

---

20. Annual returns only could be made with approval of the tax commissioner. Act 150, P. A. 1953, as amended, R. 205.551.

21. Permission to file an annual return only was extended primarily to small taxpayers. See remarks by Clarence W. Lock, "An Administrator's Point of View of the Value Added Tax," in *Alternatives to Present Federal Taxes*, a Symposium Conducted by the Tax Institute of America, Inc. (Princeton: Tax Institute of America, 1964), p. 62.

22. According to a 1963 study on the federal corporation income tax, as the income size of a business increases, cost of compliance as a percentage of business (net) income decreases, that is, the compliance burden decreases. Kenneth Stanton Johnston, *Corporations' Federal Income Tax Compliance Costs* (Columbus: Ohio State Bureau of Business Research, 1963), pp. 74–81.

ministration and ease of taxpayer compliance.[23] According to Michigan Department of Treasury officials, the cost of the administration of the BAT was lower than that of most state income taxes,[24] and administrative considerations should not be a serious factor in any decision regarding the merits of the BAT, or value-added, type of tax.[25]

Neutrality

In the context of business taxation, *neutrality* refers to the effect of taxes on the allocation of resources. In particular, neutrality requires that taxes should accomplish certain assigned objectives (for example, the distribution of tax costs in some intended pattern), but that they should not interfere with economic decisions such as those regarding the input mix, type of business organization, or capital structure which would be made in the absence of the tax.[26] A conventional yardstick for the standard of economic neutrality of business taxes is to examine the levy according to the degree of its equal application among industries and inputs. For example, a tax is neutral if it is levied generally on all types of factor incomes generated by the use of factor inputs, and thus will not directly lead to changes in the price or the quantity demanded of individual inputs and products.[27]

Capital Outlay

The original BAT statute did not permit a deduction for amortization, depletion, or depreciation allowances, or for the amount of capital asset purchases (instantaneous depreciation). An allowance for depreciation and amortization of real property was introduced into the statute in 1955 to satisfy critics who argued that since rent paid

23. See remarks by Clarence W. Lock, in "Administrative History of Michigan's Activities Tax," pp. 22–25; and T. P. Stapchinskas, "Taxation of Business in Michigan: Viewpoints of Businessmen," in *Proceedings of the Forty-Eighth Annual Conference on Taxation* (Columbus: National Tax Association, 1955), pp. 25–29.

24. Lock, Rau, and Hamilton, "The Michigan Value Added Tax," p. 366.

25. Lock, "Administrator's Point of View," p. 63.

26. Musgrave, *The Theory of Public Finance*, pp. 140–42.

27. "A tax which meets this description would be a value-added tax with no exemptions whatsoever and with all activities and all factors of production subject to the same rate of taxation." Dick Netzer, *Economics of the Property Tax*, pp. 26, 71.

was a statutory deduction from gross receipts, the denial of a depreciation deduction unfairly discriminated in favor of renters *vis-à-vis* owners of tangible assets, particularly buildings.[28] In drafting regulations defining this deduction, depletion allowance deductions still were not permitted because they were "not within legislative intent."[29] A deduction for the depreciation of personal property continued to be disallowed by the legislature for a practical reason. It was feared that since large manufacturers employed various methods for computation, including the new accelerated depreciation authorized under the 1954 U.S. Internal Revenue Code, there would be an unknown and substantial revenue loss.[30]

In addition to creating administrative problems for the Department of Treasury,[31] the differential treatment of tangible property depreciation violated the criteria for neutrality. In effect, the BAT discriminated on the basis of ownership of real versus personal property, favoring the former. The practical result would be to encourage the rental rather than purchase of items such as office equipment, automobiles and trucks, machinery, tools, and similar items. Furthermore, because of the combination of the rent paid deduction and the new allowance for real property depreciation, the BAT continued to discriminate against owners *vis-à-vis* renters of personal property, and thus only partially eliminated the source of the original criticism.

In addition to the implications of the differential treatment of real

---

28. Act 150, P. A. 1953, 205.551 and R. 205.561, Rule 11. The original statute and the subsequent criticism is discussed in Lock, Rau, and Hamilton, "The Michigan Value Added Tax," p. 360 and 360n.

29. Ibid.

30. T. W. Siedman, "Something New in Taxation," *Michigan Business Review* 7 (March 1954): 23–28; and Gornick, *The Michigan Business Receipts Tax*, pp. 16–17.

31. The Michigan Department of Treasury permitted businesses to use the same depreciation accounting methods for the BAT that they employed for federal tax purposes unless the particular type of deduction was "inconsistent with the intent" of the BAT act (R. 205.561, Rule 11). For example, a deduction for depreciation of the capitalization of payroll expenditures was not permitted since payrolls are specifically included in the BAT base. The differential treatment of tangible asset depreciation created administrative problems regarding the definition of real versus personal property. For example, is machinery which is so large that it becomes part of the building real or personal property? Is a pipeline real or personal property? These kinds of problems caused revenue officials to make recommendations that all depreciation allowances either be allowed or disallowed as statutory deductions. Michigan Department of Treasury, Revenue Division, *Annual Report*, 1958, pp. 65–66.

and personal property, the statute also violated the original intent of the BAT: "Adjusted receipts . . . shall mean the gross receipts from business less such costs as may have been incurred in the conduct of business from which receipts were derived."[32] According to the bulletin of the American Institute of Certified Public Accountants:

> Depreciation accounting . . . aims to distribute the cost or other basic value of tangible capital assets, less salvage (if any), over the estimated useful life of the unit (which may be a group of assets) in a systematic and rational manner. It is a process of allocation, not of valuation. Depreciation for the year is the portion of the total charge under such a system that is allocated to the year.[33]

This definition for all tangible assets not only questions the view that depreciation is a provision for replacement, but also places depreciation in the category of a recurrent business cost.[34]

Despite the view that a depletion allowance for natural resources was not the intent of the 1955 amendment permitting an allowance for real depreciation, a similar case can be made for cost depletion as a legitimate form of business expense which should be deducted under the provisions of the BAT. That is, because cost depletion allowances cease when the recognized value of the asset has been recovered, the process is the same as depreciation.[35]

Other Property Incomes

Both interest and dividends received were excluded from gross receipts, but only interest paid was a statutory deduction. The net result was to ignore the practical similarity of these payments regarding

---

32. Act 150, P. A. 1953, R. 205.561, Rule 11.

33. American Institute of Certified Public Accountants, *Accounting Research and Terminology Bulletins — Fiscal Edition* (New York: the Institute, 1961), Bulletin No. 1.

34. Similarly, amortization is regarded as an amortized cost. Although this is an accounting view, it is consistent with the economic viewpoint that an element of business cost is the payment for resources purchased or hired by the firm. For a discussion of the accounting aspects of depreciation and amortization as systematic costs, see J. D. Coughlan and W. K. Strand, *Depreciation: Accounting, Taxes and Business Decisions* (New York: Ronald Press, 1969), esp. pp. 1-2 through 1-8.

35. The controversial aspect of depletion centers on the alternative of percentage depletion available to owners of mineral properties. Percentage depletion allowances continue as long as the property is productive even after the recognized cost of the asset has been written off through prior allowances.

the problem of attracting capital, and, therefore, to discriminate against equity financing in favor of debt financing in much the same manner as a net income tax. The justification for special treatment of interest income and payments was that it was taxed under the Michigan intangibles statutes. On the other hand, dividends paid were nondeductible because they did not constitute an "ordinary and necessary business expense."[36] This argument for differential treatment was rather weak since interest and dividend income both were subject to the intangibles tax, and dividends, but not interest payments, were included in the adjusted receipts base of the payer. Therefore, although interest was not within the scope of the BAT, dividends were taxed at the source.

Dual Rate Structure

The reason given for taxing public utilities at preferentially lower rates was that "utilities incur expenses out of proportion to gross receipts compared to other business," and that, by their legal status, public utilities are subject to government regulations in the establishment of their service charges.[37] Nonetheless, under a comprehensive business levy there is little substantive justification for treating utilities more favorably than other types of business. If, indeed, it is true that utilities have unusually high expenses and also are artificially constrained with respect to profitability, then it also is obvious that their adjusted receipts tax base, and their tax liability, is correspondingly less.

Neutrality and Industrial Organization

Although by definition the BAT was levied on all business activities (other than those specifically excluded) regardless of size, type, or legal organization, the practical effect of the combination of the various deduction provisions and the specific dollar exemption was to eliminate many unincorporated and small firms (especially farms and personal service trades) from the coverage of the tax. The justification was that the trade-off for this treatment was reduced costs of government administration and taxpayer compliance. It is important to note here this strict neutrality violation was not necessarily undesirable. The elimination of small taxpayers from the scope of the BAT

---

36. Act 301, P. A. 1939. Act 150, P. A. 1953, Sec. 205.561, Rule 11.
37. Gornick, *The Michigan Business Receipts Tax,* p. 14.

had positive political appeal (an important consideration in tax policy) as well as the economic justification of reduced costs of administration and compliance.

A second violation of the objectives that all "business activities engaged in [in Michigan, whether interstate or intrastate] . . . with the object of gain" should be taxed under the BAT statute was due to the specific organization exemption for financial institutions.[38] This special treatment was owing to federal law, which restricted state taxation of national banks to tax paid shares, dividends derived on the taxable income of the owner or shareholder, or net income.[39] Since an adjusted receipts tax could not legally be applied to national banks, the Michigan legislature was reluctant to tax state banks differently.[40]

An economic consequence of this special exemption for financial business was the erosion of the adjusted receipts base due to the Michigan treatment of rent. Rent received was specifically included in the BAT definition of gross receipts, and a deduction was permitted for rent paid. Although the effect was to tax rent in the adjusted receipts of the payee and not the payer (thus tending to include it in the aggregate tax base), it was excluded from the scope of the BAT if it was paid to financial institutions.[41]

---

38. *Financial business* was defined as having assets of which at least 90 percent were intangible personal property and gross income of which at least 90 percent was interest or other charges resulting from the use of money or credit and dividends (Act 150, P.A. 1953, Sec. 205.551, as amended). This would include banks, trust companies, building and loan associations, and other state or federally chartered financial institutions.

39. Michigan taxed on the basis of tax paid share. Other financial institutions pay similar intangibles taxes (Act 301, P. A. 1939).

40. Firmin, *Business Receipts Tax*, p. 23. Even if federal law had permitted taxing the adjusted receipts of financial institutions under the BAT there would have been perplexing problems of computing adjusted receipts, in particular, the treatment of rent and interest components, which are considered in the following sources: M. Bronfenbrenner, "The Japanese Value-Added Sales Tax," *National Tax Journal* 3 (1950): 303 ff. and Table 1-B, pp. 352–53; and Sullivan, *Tax on Value Added*, pp. 205–209. Of course, in strict terms the problem of interest would not arise in the case of the BAT's application to financial institutions since, as was discussed in a preceding section, interest was excluded *de facto* from the adjusted receipts base. Effective 1 January 1973, a national bank may be treated for tax purposes as a bank organized under the existing laws of the state or other jurisdiction within which its principle office is located. This liberalization of federal law paves the way for increased taxes on state as well as nationally chartered banks (P. L. 91-156 [1969] and P. L. 92-213 [1971]).

41. Similarly, rent paid to nonprofit institutions which also were exempt from the BAT was excluded from the taxable base.

10

Economic

Effects of the Tax

In public finance discussions of the economic effects of a particular state business tax, three practical questions inevitably arise. In what direction is the tax shifted from point of impact, that is, will it result in higher prices to consumers or lower returns to factor suppliers? Are in-state residents likely to pay it? What will be the effect of the tax on the state's economic growth?

These first two questions are important to an understanding of the nature of a tax since their determination is a necessary first step in the examination of how the fiscal process may affect the ultimate distribution of income and wealth. Furthermore, in the justification of state business taxation it is necessary to know to what degree tax costs of businesses are ultimately borne by those individuals who, through the vehicle of the business enterprise, benefit from the public services of tax jurisdictions in which they do not reside.

The third issue, the influence a state tax may exert on industry location decisions and, therefore, on the growth of the economic base of a state, has long-term implications not only for the living standard (per capita incomes) of individuals residing within the tax jurisdiction, but also for future budgetary processes. If, for example, a particular tax is found to have an important negative influence on business location choices, the tax jurisdiction which levies that tax not only will be restricting the future income of its citizens, but also, by constraining the growth of the tax base, will be defeating the primary purpose of state taxes, namely, to raise revenues. As a result, the state will be forcing its citizens either to accept fewer public goods and services, or to add increasing tax burdens through tax rate and/or base changes in order merely to keep pace with the horizontal growth requirements of public goods.

Finally, although all of these issues are economic rather than political, the politico-legislative implications are most important from a state tax policy point of view; it is likely that a state legislature's understanding (or misunderstanding) of these issues will play a major role in the practical consideration of a particular tax. Accordingly, information on these issues must be provided in order that informed policy judgments may be made.

Tax Shifting

For cases in which the concepts of business tax impact (legal monetary obligation of the taxpaying unit) and the tax incidence (ultimate impact or obligation) differ, the tax is said to be shifted. A business tax may be shifted either forward to consumers in the form of higher product prices, or backward to factor suppliers through a reduction in the prices paid by the firm for its inputs.[1] Identification of the extent to which a tax may be shifted forward or backward from the point of initial impact is a function of many determinants;[2] for each of these, a multiplicity of variables will influence the final result. The problem requires arranging experiments in which all elements other than those being specifically considered for their effect remain unchanged. As a result, these questions of shifting present formidable analytical and conceptual problems.[3]

---

1. Impact and incidence were discussed in chapter 6.

2. Some important determinants are: behavioral assumptions regarding maximization objectives of individuals and businesses, market structure, price elasticity of final demand, price elasticities of resource supply, technology, degree of specialization of inputs, and so on. For a discussion of the analysis of various determinants in the open economy, see Charles McLure, "Commodity Tax Incidence in Open Economies," *National Tax Journal* 17 (June 1964): 187 ff.

3. In an effort to explicitly specify these problems, econometric methods recently have been applied to the shifting issue. However, the results are just as inconclusive as the noneconometric techniques. For example, regarding the

In discussing the shifting of the BAT, three major criteria used to identify the direction of business tax shifting will be presented, and their relationship to the BAT will be evaluated. In order to isolate these issues, the analysis is made in a short-run partial equilibrium framework. All economic variables, except those otherwise specified, are assumed to be unchanged. It is of importance to note that the focus in the subsequent discussion is on the economic nature of the BAT and the conditions affecting shifting which are unique to the Michigan economy. No analysis is made of many other admittedly important economic factors.

Determinants

The conventional approach to a discussion of the shifting of the BAT has been to recognize it as a form of value-added tax and then to draw the analogy between the ease of forward shifting of a single stage retail sales tax and the BAT.[4] In a closed economy context

---

shifting of the federal corporate income tax, Krzyzaniak and Musgrave (K-M) conclude that there is more than 100 percent forward shifting. These results have been criticized by a number of writers, including Cragg, Harberger, and Mieszkowski, who conclude that "capital bears approximately the full burden of the tax" (p. 821). See Marian Krzyzaniak and Richard A. Musgrave, *The Shifting of the Corporation Income Tax* (Baltimore: Johns Hopkins Press, 1963); and John G. Cragg, Arnold C. Harberger, and Peter Mieszkowski, "Empirical Evidence on the Incidence of the Corporation Income Tax," *Journal of Political Economy* 75 (December 1967): 811–21. Slitor also has questioned the results of the K-M model and presents an excellent review and discussion on the state of the art of shifting analysis in general. Richard E. Slitor, "Corporate Tax Incidence: Economic Adjustments to Differentials under a Two Tier Tax Structure," in *Effects of the Corporation Income Tax*, edited by Marian Krzyzaniak (Detroit: Wayne State University Press, 1966), pp. 136–206. The issue is reviewed by Peter Mieszkowski in "Tax Incidence Theory: The Effects of Taxes on the Distribution of Income," *Journal of Economic Literature* 7 (December 1969): 1116–1121.

4. This view of state value-added taxes is suggested by Charles F. Bonser, who notes that there are "few dissenters to the concept of full forward shifting of the value-added tax." See "Evaluation of a Tax on Value Added and Possible Application in Indiana," in *Business Taxation in Indiana* (Indianapolis: Indiana Commission on State Tax and Financing Policy, 1966), pp. 103–104; Richard Slitor, "The Role of Value Added in the Tax Structure of the States: Prospective Developments," in *Proceedings of the Sixty-First Annual Conference on Taxation* (Columbus: National Tax Association, 1968), pp. 110, 114; and Sullivan, *Tax on Value Added*, p. 304 and 304n. Sullivan notes that the "prevailing opinion" regarding the BAT is to "assume forward shifting as under a sales tax."

such a conclusion seems plausible because of the accounting equivalence of value added and the sales bases. However, this forward shifting assumption merits further examination, first because tax base equivalence does not necessarily imply similar economic effects, and, second, because the criteria or determinants of shifting will differ in the open versus closed framework. The three determinants to be considered are the cost nature of the tax, the size of the tax base, and the relationship of the taxed industry to the extent of the final market in which it operates. The first two determinants hold for business taxes imposed by national as well as subnational economies, the third specifically draws attention to shifting within the structure of the open economy.[5]

Cost Nature of the Tax. Businesses shift tax costs. If a tax is levied on a variable cost base, it is more easily shifted forward than is a fixed cost or lump sum type tax such as a corporation franchise fee. That is, in contrast to taxes which are paid regardless of the level of a firm's production or the height of final product price, taxes such as the BAT, which vary directly with the amount of private inputs used (such as labor and tangible personal property), affect the total variable cost of production and, consequently, the post-tax price–output levels. The degree of this forward shifting, of course, ultimately will depend on the price elasticity conditions of resource supply and final product demand.

Size of the Tax Base. The broader the base of the tax, that is, the more uniformly it is levied on the production or use of a wide range of inputs or products, the less easily it is shifted backward. When the tax base is narrow there is likely to be a substitution effect away from the base taxed and toward the use of available and untaxed substitutes. It is this factor which leads even critics of state levied, value-added taxes such as the BAT to rate them higher than their principal competitor — the corporation income tax — regarding the certainty of tax shifting.[6]

Relationship to Final Market. A prime determinant of the direction of shifting of any business tax levied within an open economy is the relationship between the various industries and the extent of the final market. A tax levied on an industry selling primarily intrastate

---

5. These determinants are a combination of those suggested by Charles E. McLure, "The Interstate Exporting of State and Local Taxes: Estimates for 1962," *National Tax Journal* 20 (March 1967): 56–59; Carl S. Shoup, *Public Finance*, pp. 7–10; and Netzer, *Property Tax*, pp. 111–12.

6. Slitor, "Role of Value Added," pp. 109–110.

is likely to be shifted forward if the industry's product does not face substitution competition from untaxed industries operating either within or without the state.[7] The criteria are qualitatively similar for firms operating in regional or national markets. Other things being equal, business taxes on firms competing with out-of-state untaxed industries probably cannot be shifted forward unless the firm dominates production of its particular product. State taxed industries facing these competitors in a national sales framework have no alternative in the short run but to absorb taxes in reduced payments to factors, most likely profits.[8] If the state taxed industry dominates the national or regional market and, for practical purposes, determines final price–output relationships, then forward shifting is likely to occur, even for taxes levied on a relatively narrow tax base (such as profits taxes).[9]

Given the first two criteria for shifting — variable costs and width of tax base — the BAT has the merits of a tax capable of being easily shifted forward. It is necessary to apply the third criterion for shifting, namely, the relationship of a taxed industry to the rest of the economy, in order to reach conclusions in the context of the structure of the Michigan economy. Using this criterion, the following statements regarding the direction of shifting of the BAT may be made.

• The major industry groups of construction, utilities, wholesale trade, and retail trade would have been able to shift the BAT forward onto their final product prices. This would have been possible because these industries operate primarily within the economy of the state of Michigan and, in addition, do not face competition from untaxed in-state or out-of-state firms offering substitute products.[10]

---

7. For example, given this criteria it is concluded that due to the nature of its legally protected monopoly position, a state's public utilities, including local transportation and communications firms, would have little difficulty passing the BAT along to consumers. McLure, "Interstate Exporting," p. 57.

8. Ibid, p. 57. This is because capital is largely committed in the short run, and therefore less mobile and more supply inelastic than in the long run.

9. A state industry dominates the national market if it accounts for as much as 40 percent of national value added in that industry. This threshold is reduced to 25 percent to account for market structure for industries in which the largest 4 firms produce as much as 50 percent of national value added. Using these criteria, Michigan's transportation equipment sector (which had more than 97 percent of value added from motor vehicles and equipment) dominated its market. Ibid., p. 58, and *Annual Survey of Manufacturers*, 1964-65.

10. Based on data computed from John L. Hazard, *Michigan's Commerce: Domestic and International*, Technical Report No. 5 (Lansing: Michigan Department of Commerce, 1966), esp. pp. 23–30, 62.

• The agriculture and service trade industries, although primarily operating within the state market, would have had difficulty in shifting the tax forward. For agriculture, the reason is twofold. First, in an agricultural import state such as Michigan, the competition from untaxed out-of-state agricultural industries is a factor which makes forward shifting difficult.[11] Second, even if Michigan were not an agricultural importer, more than one-third of total gross receipts generated by in-state agricultural firms would be exempt through the statutory deduction and specific dollar exemption provisions.[12] Taxed Michigan firms (mostly corporate) would face price effect competition from untaxed Michigan agricultural products (mostly noncorporate) as well as from imports. The argument that Michigan service trades would have short-run difficulty in shifting the BAT is the same as the second reason presented for agricultural business (that is, a large number of competing trade establishments are exempt).[13]

• Unlike other major industry groups subject to the BAT, the mining and manufacturing industries operate in national product markets. To the extent that these Michigan businesses face price competition from out-of-state untaxed firms, do not have certain production cost advantages *vis-à-vis* these competitors due to location proximity of customers, and do not dominate the final market, forward shifting of the BAT would have been difficult. Within this context, there are three important considerations: (1) a recent study by the Advisory Commission on Intergovernmental Relations (ACIR) concludes that subnational tax policies tend to neutralize each other in terms of tax costs on business,[14] thus reducing (not eliminating) the importance of state taxes as a price determining factor among competing firms; (2) Table 28, which indicates the importance of the apportioned BAT base for multistate business attributable to the sales destination versus the property and payroll factors, indicates that the Michigan stone, clay, and glass, primary metals, and electrical machine industries made a large percentage of sales within Michigan. While these industries do not dominate national markets, it is likely that they have location cost advantages over out-of-state competitors; and (3),

---

11. Ibid., Exhibit XV, p. 62.

12. Chapter 9, Table 30.

13. Ibid. This is true at least for the firms which are just large enough to be taxable, but are unable to take advantage of any economies of scale or other cost reducing factors unavailable to exempt business.

14. Advisory Commission on Intergovernmental Relations, *State-Local Taxation and Industrial Location*, pp. 63–66.

because Michigan transportation equipment manufacturing dominates its national market (motor vehicles), this industry probably could have shifted the BAT forward.

Conclusion. Based on the criteria for determining the direction of shifting and the classifications of various industries according to these criteria, the following industries would have been able, for various reasons, to shift much of the BAT forward: construction, utilities, wholesale trade, retail trade and, within manufacturing, transportation equipment, stone, clay and glass, primary metals, and electrical machinery. These industries accounted for more than 60 percent of total BAT collections.

Finally, but most important, it should again be noted that this discussion is focused on the tax element on final price effects, and that there are a host of other economic factors which influence the direction of business tax shifting, especially for firms operating in national markets. For example, the variables of technology, efficiency of management, mobility and productivity of factors, importance of market location externalities, nature of market structure, and even the extent to which national monetary policy permits increases in the general price level determine the ability of businesses to shift taxes. Although the discussion of the determinants of tax shifting is useful, especially as it applies to the open economy, it should be kept in mind that factors other than taxes, particularly for firms operating in national markets, ultimately may determine the direction of shift.[15]

An Administered Pricing Policy

The previous discussion regarding tax shifting determinants accepted the assumption that businessmen were able to compute their BAT liability on a given transaction and, if feasible, mark up final market prices accordingly. However, since the BAT was computed quarterly and/or annually, it was, as a practical matter, quite unlikely that a businessman had any knowledge of the percentage of his gross receipts which would be represented by his adjusted receipts base. Even with this knowledge, businessmen would not have had information on the tax base–gross receipts relationship of their in- or out-of-state competitors. Most probably, after experiencing the BAT for a year or two the business accounting departments of firms began to

---

15. This point also provides a somewhat negative justification for concentrating on the impact rather than the incidence of business taxes.

determine an average percentage of the BAT liability to gross receipts and, if the market demand conditions permitted, to add that percentage to final market prices of their goods and services.

M. Bronfenbrenner suggests that such a pricing policy is the expected outcome under a tax computed as gross receipts less interfirm purchases (such as a value-added or adjusted receipts type base),[16] and that the tax shifting behavior of the generally known representative firm ultimately will determine the degree of tax shifting among its competitors. Those firms whose ratio of the tax base to gross receipts is higher than that of the representative firm will be unable to pass the tax on in full. On the other hand, those firms having a ratio lower than that of the representative firm among their competitors may be able to pass on more than a full amount.[17] This reasoning is useful in a discussion of the BAT only to the extent that, within the open economy framework, the non-BAT taxpaying competitors have similar tax impact levels and problems in determining their tax base–gross receipts relationship.

Exporting Tax Costs

In discussing the rationale for the BAT the point was made that, due to the openness of state economies, individuals as consumers or factor suppliers derive benefits from business enterprises operating in a given state even if those individuals are nonresidents of the state to which the business activity can be attributed. This reasoning provided the conceptual basis for the justification of state business taxation, namely, that taxing income at its source is the only procedure available for assessing individuals, wherever they may reside, for benefits of public services accruing initially to the business entity.

To the extent that the BAT was shifted, forward or backward, to residents of jurisdictions other than Michigan, the tax was exported.[18] One basis for determining the amount of the BAT exported would be to identify the extent to which the tax was shifted to the three factors

---

16. M. Bronfenbrenner, "The Japanese Value-Added Sales Tax," pp. 310–11.

17. Ibid., p. 310.

18. Ideally, in a context of fiscal federalism, a state business tax would be designed to match the benefit (of public services) export with tax cost export. For a discussion of this point see Richard A. Musgrave and Peggy Brewer Richman, "Allocation Aspects, Domestic and International," in *The Role of Direct and Indirect Taxes,* pp. 98–99.

in the multistate allocation formula (sales, property, payroll) which were used to apportion total adjusted receipts between Michigan and other states.[19] For example, the part of the BAT shifted backward to payrolls would be absorbed primarily by Michigan's labor residents, and the part shifted to the property factor would be paid by land and capital owners, some of whom reside outside Michigan.[20]

On the other hand, to the extent that the BAT was shifted forward to sales (determined either by the firm–market relationship or by administered pricing techniques discussed on pages 139–40), the tax, *ceteris paribus,* would be divided between Michigan and non-Michigan residents on the basis of the proportion of total Michigan business shipments to out-of-state markets. Given this criterion, and assuming full forward shifting, the following industries would have been the major vehicles for BAT exporting:[21] agriculture (40.8 percent); mining (46.7 percent); food and kindred products (68.4 percent); textile mills (95.0 percent); furniture and fixtures (69.2 percent); printing and publishing (44.7 percent); chemicals and allied products (81.8 percent); rubber and plastics (47.2 percent); stone, clay, and glass (40.7 percent); fabricated metals (73.6 percent); machinery, except electrical (82.3 percent); electrical machinery (89.6 percent); and miscellaneous manufacturing (71.6 percent). Michigan manufacturing exports 82.1 percent of its total value of shipments to markets outside the state.

In a 1958 tax study by Richard Musgrave and Darwin Daicoff, assumptions were made as to the probable direction of tax shifting for three state business sectors (automobile manufacturing, all other manufacturing, and nonmanufacturing), and as to the degree of relative importance of the sales-property-payroll factors in the inter-

---

19. The government's desire to export taxes to other jurisdictions suggests that an origin rather than destination principle be adopted for levying a value-added type tax. See discussion by McLure, "The Value Added Tax."

20. To the extent that large manufacturing labor unions had strong economic bargaining power in Michigan, and thus were able to maintain wage rigidity in a downward direction, backward shifting of the BAT to wage earners would have been especially difficult. For comments on this factor see William Haber, Eugene C. McKean, and Harold C. Taylor, *The Michigan Economy: Its Potentials and Its Problems* (Kalamazoo: Upjohn Institute for Employment Research, 1959), Appendix A.

21. Figures in parentheses indicate percentage of total shipments made. Estimates computed from Hazard, *Michigan's Commerce,* Exhibit XV. Data are for 1960.

state alteration formula of these sectors.[22] To illustrate, for all non-automobile manufacturers the entire sales portion of the total BAT base plus 10 percent of the payroll component of the BAT base was assumed to be shifted forward to Michigan consumers; 50 percent of the payroll portion of the tax base was assumed shifted backward to Michigan wage earners. The remaining 40 percent was treated as a profits tax and distributed on the basis of the residence of dividend recipients. The BAT payment attributable to the property factor was also handled by this profits tax approach. Given these assumptions, the conclusion of the study is that approximately 26 percent of the (1956) BAT payments were exported from Michigan.[23]

Taxation and Industry Location

One of the most debated issues in state public finance is the influence of state and local tax policy on the location decisions of businesses.[24] The issue is important because the location of new industry within a tax jurisdiction leads to increased tax bases (either directly as the number of businesses increases, or indirectly as a result of personal incomes originating in business) as well as to higher employment and growth levels for the state in which the business operates.[25] Accordingly, if state and local business taxes can be shown to discourage existing firms from expanding or new firms from entering, then policy decisions designed to promote state economic growth must consider changes in the level and/or structure of the existing system. Despite the many other merits of a particular tax, if legisla-

---

22. Richard A. Musgrave and Darwin W. Daicoff, "Who Pays Michigan Taxes?" in *Michigan Tax Study Papers*, pp. 142–43, and 178-79. This article presents allocation methods for all three sectors.

23. Ibid., Table 2, p. 135.

24. For a survey, see John F. Due, "Studies of State–Local Tax Influences," pp. 163–73.

25. At least four types of location decisions affect the economic growth of a state: (1) the establishment of new firms, usually small; (2) the decision of an existing firm to remain in a state or locate elsewhere; (3) the decision of existing firms to expand within or without the state; and (4) the decision of an expanding out-of-state firm to locate in a state. Eva Mueller, Arnold Wilken, and Margaret Wood, *Location Decisions and Industrial Mobility in Michigan* (Ann Arbor: University of Michigan Institute for Social Research, 1961), p. 19. It should be recognized that relocation of business entails large costs and rarely will occur. Of far greater importance are decisions regarding establishment of new firms or expansion of old ones.

tors conclude that it has an actual or potential negative influence on the state's industrial development, that levy probably will be rejected.

The General Issue

The issue of state taxes and interstate effects is as perennial as it is important. When the first state corporation income tax was enacted in Wisconsin in 1911, it was announced that Ringling Brothers of Baraboo were moving out of the state due to the tax.[26] Since then, criticism of business taxes has continued from the business sector, generally on the basis of interstate tax level differentials. For example, in a 1961 study by the Survey Research Center of the University of Michigan, manufacturers were invited to comment on the effects of Michigan's business taxes on their expansion decisions. The consensus of those critical of the structure was that the level of taxes paid by business in the state was too high, but there were only a few comments regarding the effects of particular tax levies.[27] Similarly, in a 1960 collection of papers written by various business officials and tax experts on Michigan taxes and economic growth, there was considerable agreement that, compared to other states, taxes on businesses in Michigan were relatively heavy. Some suggested that state business taxes in general should be reduced, or, at least, not increased further.[28]

On the other hand, students of state budget policy cite research which concludes there is no significant correlation between interstate tax differentials and location and/or expansion decisions.[29] Similarly, most studies which have examined those factors influencing industrial location decisions have concluded that the primary considerations are economic, for example, availability of labor, proximity to final markets or specialized resources, and transportation costs, rather

---

26. *Madison Democrat*, 12 April 1912, cited in *Wisconsin's State and Local Tax Burden*, p. 27.

27. Mueller, Wilken, and Wood, *Location Decisions*, pp. 36–40.

28. McCracken, ed., *Taxes and Economic Growth*, pp. 9–11; Maurice Fulton, "Michigan's Tax Structure and Its Influence on Economic Development," and Harold Groves, "Michigan's Taxes and Economic Growth," both in *Taxes and Economic Growth*, pp. 75 and 97, respectively.

29. For example, see Due, "Studies of State–Local Tax Influence," pp. 167–77; and Eva Mueller and James N. Morgan, "Location Decisions of Manufacturers," *American Economic Review, Papers and Proceedings* 52 (May 1962): 206–17.

than financial, for example, taxes and state industrial incentives.[30]

In short, firms locate where they can find that combination of land, labor, and capital which will permit profit maximization, and the state–local tax cost element is only of secondary importance. This appears to be true for small as well as large businesses.

> [An] overemphasized [locational] factor is tax considerations. Between States, tax considerations have tended to level off. Whereas some States have gross volume taxes, and others income taxes, the net collected from most businesses tends to be the same. On rare occasions, some significant differences occur because of the peculiarities of some companies, but these are not necessarily permanent, and successive legislatures can change regulations at will. And . . . among the factors that are increasing in importance are labor considerations, market considerations, and financing arrangements. Among those that are decreasing in importance are tax considerations, unionization, and raw material access.[31]

Even relatively high levels of business taxation do not have a major influence on location decisions. While the analysis of location factors is not conclusive, studies indicate that tax levels are of minor importance.[32]

Industrial Location Studies

Most analyses of state tax influences on industrial location decisions are based on the implicit assumption that there are, in fact, intraregional interstate tax cost differentials which (in combination with the direction of shifting) will determine a state's location competitiveness.[33] In order to examine this interstate tax differential question the

---

30. For example, see Due, "Studies of State–Local Tax Influences"; Mueller and Morgan, "Location Decisions"; Haber, McKean, and Taylor, *Michigan Economy*, chap. 6; M. D. Greenhut and Marshall R. Colberg, *Factors in the Location of Florida Industry* (Tallahassee: The Florida State University, 1962), esp. pp. 58–81; and M. L. Greenhut, *Plant Location in Theory and Practice* (Chapel Hill: University of North Carolina Press, 1955).

31. Fred I. Weber, Jr., *Locating or Relocating Your Business*, a Report Prepared for the Small Business Administration (Washington, D.C.: U.S. Government Printing Office, June 1969), p. 5.

32. Due, "Studies of State–Local Tax Influences," p. 171.

33. During the period of the BAT three major studies dealt specially with the effect of the Michigan tax structure on business location decisions. (1) The Upjohn Institute for Employment Research report agreed that Michigan was a high business tax state, and some contributors warned in general terms against

ACIR analyzed the business tax structure by U.S. regions of neighboring states characterized by sharp differences in employment growth rates. The hypothesis to be tested was that if industrial location trends were definitely shaped by relatively low state and local taxes, this effect should be most discernible for states within the same region.[34]

The business tax system of the state in each region which showed the greatest growth in manufacturing employment between 1950 and 1965 was compared with the tax system of the state in the same region registering the lowest growth rate during that period. State tax systems were compared on the basis of total business tax collections as a percentage of personal income originating in the state business sector. The results indicated that since tax costs differentials among states with differing rates of growth were so small, it could be concluded "that there [was] no clear cut relationship between the level of business taxes and manufacturing employment growth rates for states within the same region."[35]

---

a tendency to dismiss the significance of taxation on industrial location decisions. However, there was no consensus as to which business taxes, if any, should be changed or repealed. (2) The *Michigan Tax Study* emphasized that location decisons are affected by tax levels only if there are interstate tax differentials, and only if these differentials reduce profits through backward shifting. (Given this view, the conclusion that the bulk of the BAT is forward shifted suggests that the BAT would not directly affect location choices.) Other economic considerations such as transport charges, high labor productivity, proximity to raw materials, and tax exporting would take precedence over tax levels in location decisions. The conclusion was reached that state business taxes are in most instances insignificant if not negligible elements in the total cost structure of the business firm. (3) The University of Michigan study used a sample survey approach. Its comparison of Michigan and Ohio businesses in 1961 with a similar study for 1950 indicated that in 1950 only 9 percent of businesses said Michigan taxes were a negative factor (*vis-à-vis* Ohio) in location decisions; in 1961, 58 percent said taxes were a disadvantage. The tax most often singled out as adversely affecting plant location was the local property tax. See McCracken, ed., *Taxes and Economic Growth*, p. 167; Wolfgang F. Stolper, "Economic Development, Taxation, and Industrial Location in Michigan," in *Michigan Tax Study Papers*, chap. 2; Mueller, Wilken, and Wood, *Location Decisions*, p. 115; *Industrial Mobility in Michigan* (Ann Arbor: University of Michigan Institute for Social Research, 1950), pp. 77; and Paul. W. McCracken, "Taxes and Michigan's Economic Problems," in *The Michigan Economy: Prospects and Problems* (Kalamazoo: Upjohn Institute, 1962), p. 46.

34. Advisory Commission on Intergovernmental Relations, *State–Local Taxation and Industrial Location*, pp. 59–77. The region included Michigan, Ohio, Indiana, Illinois, and Wisconsin.

35. Ibid., p. 66.

Of particular interest is the ACIR's finding that although this growth–business tax cost test does not support the contention that the state and local tax factor represents an insignificant cost element of businesses, it does suggest that there are tax neutralization policies pursued by neighboring states which tend to eliminate state tax differentials as factors in industrial location decisions.

> Just as the executives of multistate firms are becoming increasingly sensitive to variations in interstate cost factors, so also are State tax policymakers becoming increasingly concerned about the industrial location implications of interstate tax differentials. In order to be on the safe side, State tax policymakers have developed a neutralization system that has at least two distinctive characteristics — the direct matching and trade-off approaches. With the direct matching approach a State attempts to stay in line with its neighbors on a tax by tax basis; . . . under a trade-off system [a state offsets] an unfavorable tax situation (high rate) in one tax category with a favorable tax situation (a lower rate or no tax) in another.[36]

Although taxes are considered a not insignificant element in the overall cost structure of the firm, they cannot be considered of major importance in industrial location decisions and, therefore, are not an important negative factor in economic growth. In general, fears of state legislators that business taxes will drive business out are not well founded. However, until legislators are given information regarding the nature of this issue, tax changes will continue to be made on the basis of supposed negative effects on location choices, and these changes, more often than not, will center around adjustments in the state business tax structure.[37]

The BAT and Industrial Location

The appraisal by various public finance analysts of the effect of the BAT on industrial location and economic growth in Michigan was mixed. Recommendations ranged from outright repeal (and, usually, replacement by a corporate net income tax) to conclusions that the BAT be maintained as an integral part of the state's revenue system, but that it be modified to conform more nearly to the structure of a pure value-added tax. Despite these and other conclusions and rec-

---

36. Ibid.
37. Bahl and Shellhammer, "Fiscal Planning and State Business Taxation," p. 418.

ommendations, the various criteria which were suggested for judging state tax effects on location decisions were applied to the entire Michigan state and local structure rather than to specific tax levies.

In order to analyze the specific role which the BAT, as one element of the Michigan fiscal structure, had on location decisions, it is necessary to explicitly identify various tax-oriented location determinants or criteria, and to examine the extent to which the BAT was consistent with these. If it can be shown, for example, that the decision to locate or expand business facilities is positively affected by certain tax characteristics, and that the BAT possessed these, then the tax can be counted as having had a favorable effect on location choices. Conversely, if the BAT does not exhibit these positive characteristics, then it can be said to have had a negative influence on location and, therefore, on state economic development.

BUSINESS TAX CLIMATE. The term *tax climate* for industry location and growth is periodically mentioned in discussions regarding the effects of state and local tax policy on business decisions, but it is difficult to define precisely. Used here, the term will refer to the general administrative and taxpayer (business community) attitude toward a tax, and the resulting tax image these attitudes give a state. Factory location experts regard it as having some importance.[38] One research study concluded that many firms categorically reject Michigan from consideration for location because of an unsatisfactory image, and suggested that a shift away from business taxation in general would "do much to improve the State's 'business climate,' the morale of businessmen, and increase the possibilities for industrial development and growth."[39]

Of course, opinions by businessmen on business taxes are usually easy to obtain. It would be a simple matter to provide an extensive list, both pro and con, but it can be concluded that the general reaction of Michigan businessmen and government administrators to the BAT was a favorable one.[40] Besides being relatively simple to administer and to comply with, the BAT was considered by both tax

---

38. Due, "Studies of State–Local Tax Influence," p. 169; and Fulton, "Michigan's Tax Structure," pp. 69–75.

39. Fulton, "Michigan's Tax Structure," pp. 72–75.

40. For both positions see Mueller, Wilken, and Wood, *Location Decisions*, pp. 36–40; and Dixwell L. Pierce, "State Business Taxes Not Business Barriers," *National Tax Journal* 13 (September 1960): 232–42.

economists and industry executives as conforming to rational principles of business taxation.[41]

The significance of tax climate and the resulting state tax image is difficult to assess, primarily because it often may be based more on emotion than on intellectual rationalization. Nevertheless, this emotional element can affect policy, especially since the business tax structure is the one factor which is under the direct control of legislative bodies. Finally, it should be recalled that members of the state's business community were the original writers and proponents of the tax, an important practical fact to consider in deciding whether or not the BAT (or a tax based on the general economic principle of the BAT) contributed to a negative tax image.

Tax Costs. One of the obvious economic implications of a particular tax to a firm maximizing profits is the tax's significance in the total cost structure of the business enterprise. Estimates indicate that for the highest BAT cost industries — construction and manufacturing — the figure was less than one-half of 1 percent of the total cost measure. This figure is considered low in terms of general business taxes,[42] and it can be concluded that the BAT was not one of the high cost elements in the Michigan tax system, which was characterized as "relatively heavy."[43] Indeed, the BAT at its 7¾ mill rate did not "seem to be a serious drag on economic development," and its influence on location and economic growth was "probably negligible."[44]

Distribution of Payments. When measuring structural tax payment inequalities among industry groups in Michigan, the structural distribution of business tax impact can be as important as tax levels in determining location choices. This factor is especially relevant if a state legislature concludes that the distribution pattern of a particular tax discriminates against an industry or industries believed to be important to the economic development of a state. Taxes regarded as arbitrary or unequal in their impact would be avoided in favor of those thought to distribute tax costs or tax burdens in a more equal interindustry pattern.

---

41. Professor Harold Groves referred to the BAT as "the one pioneering effort in Michigan to rationalize the tax system." Groves, "Michigan Taxes and Economic Growth," p. 92. For an alternative view see Stapchinskas, "Taxation of Business in Michigan," p. 26.

42. Stolper, "Economic Development," pp. 85–86. Also see chapters 6 and 7.

43. *Taxes and Economic Growth*, p. 10.

44. These quotes are from Buehler, "State and Local Tax Structure," p. 42; and Carl S. Shoup, "Suggested Changes," p. 161.

Based on previous data, in terms of its interindustry structural tax distribution the BAT is superior to both the gross receipts and corporate net income tax levies, but is inferior to a value-added or net income tax on total (corporate and noncorporate) business.[45] The policy implications based on the structural distribution of tax payments as an industry location determinant are that the BAT either should have been repealed in favor of a net income levy, or amended to conform to the value-added tax.

THE NO-PROFIT FIRM. The most common criticism of the BAT in the context of state tax influences on location decisions was that it was levied on business regardless of the level of profitability. When Michigan businessmen criticized the BAT as unfair, they usually referred to the fact that it was levied on a base broader than profits; the zero or negative profit firm could be forced to pay some taxes for government services.[46] This particular characteristic was considered a negative factor, especially regarding location and expansion decisions for small businesses.[47]

Despite claims that the BAT was against small business, the empirical evidence actually indicates that, due to the specific dollar exemption and statutory deduction combination, most small firms were excluded from the scope of the tax. The relevant policy conclusion is that in principle the BAT was a tax on factor incomes other than profits, but there was a practical trade-off established between the height of a specific exemption and a minimum standard deduction and the comprehensiveness of coverage of small businesses. The BAT was structured toward the first of these, and as a result did exempt many small businesses (which also account for the bulk of the no-profit businesses in Michigan).[48]

REVENUE PRODUCTIVITY. The business decision to locate or expand facilities within a particular tax jurisdiction is in every sense a commitment to a future economic climate. The more uncertain the future conditions of a particular state may appear, the less likely it is that a favorable location decision will be made. These decisions and

---

45. See chapter 7.

46. For example, see Mattersdorf, "Suggested Changes," p. 143; and Mueller, Wilken, and Wood, *Location Decisions*, pp. 39–40.

47. Mueller, Wilken, and Wood, *Location Decisions*, p. 39. Also see comments by Howard Preston, "The Michigan Business Activity Tax," p. 35.

48. U.S. Department of the Treasury, Internal Revenue Service, *Statistics of Income — 1965, U.S. Business Tax Returns* (Washington, D.C.: Government Printing Office, 1968), Tables 2-1 and 3-1.

the resulting effect on a state's economic development will be influenced as much by how business views the state's economic future as by existing conditions.

Of course, due to the inability of subnational governments to control stabilization policies affecting their economies, the major responsibility of providing a favorable investment outlook everywhere lies with the national government. The one location factor which a state, as an individual governmental unit, can influence is its fiscal structure. Since favorable industry location climate implies the minimization of future economic uncertainty, the fiscal structure must be designed to achieve that end. Such factors as periodic state financial crises, tax changes on short notice, and allowing politics to dictate tax decisions will be counted negatively in plant location decisions.

In order to reduce this negative effect the state must adopt taxes which will provide adequate revenues to meet both horizontal growth in the demand for state public services (due to factors such as population growth and rising prices), and vertical public service growth requirements (necessitated by demands for a wider scope of government services). State taxes must be income elastic.[49] Measures of the revenue characteristics of the BAT within the total Michigan structure indicate that the tax added an element of income elasticity (adequacy) in periods of expansion, and exhibited relative income inelasticity in periods of deflation.[50] Regarding the important location factor of minimization of future economic uncertainty, it can be concluded that the BAT exerted a positive influence.

IMPLICATIONS FOR ECONOMIC GROWTH. In direct contrast to the business net income tax approach, a net income or consumption value-added tax tends to encourage (or, at least, not discourage) the substitution of capital for labor. The reason for this effect is clear: a value-added tax is imposed on all factors of production used by the business firm, whereas the impact of the net income levy is directed at the return to capital.[51] Given an equal yield basis of comparison, the value-added tax, with its neutrality among alternative inputs, would be more favorable than a net income levy for the capital deepening kind

---

49. Shoup, "Suggested Changes," p. 153.
50. See chapter 5.
51. For discussion on this topic see the unpublished paper by Richard E. Slitor, "Comparative Analysis of a Value Added Tax and a Corporate Net Income Tax as State Business Taxes," presented at the Business Tax Seminar at Indiana University, Bloomington, 9 November 1967.

of investment which is associated with employment of technological advances. Relative to the conventional net income levy, the value-added tax would be conducive to investment and growth within the state.

To the extent to which the BAT achieved this neutrality among inputs, it would be counted as having had a favorable effect on state industrial location and economic growth. Although the tax was levied on payrolls as well as profits, thus ranking it above a net income levy in its positive effect on economic growth, the inconsistent statutory treatment of real versus personal property and of interest versus dividend payments (important deviations from a value-added tax structure) reduced the potentially favorable effect of the BAT on state economic development. The policy conclusion is much the same as was reached previously. The BAT would have more fully achieved its assigned objectives (in this case, with respect to industrial location choices and economic growth) had it been amended to eliminate its discriminatory treatment of certain types of capital expenditures as well as of property incomes.

Conclusion

The bulk of research examining the effect of state taxes on economic growth, which usually emphasizes interstate tax cost differentials, indicates that state tax considerations have only a minor influence on industry location and expansion choices, and, therefore, on economic development. Of far greater importance are nontax factors such as proximity to markets, availability of raw materials, productivity of labor, public service facilities, and the like. This is not to say that state taxes are completely irrelevant location factors; rather, there are other aspects of state government policy which, when taken as a whole, will exert a greater influence. To the extent that a particular tax contributes positively to state policy, it can be judged as having a net favorable influence on state development.

In particular, businessmen who make location decisions look to the future. Such governmental fiscal factors as certainty, effect of taxes on investment (for example, factor neutrality), adequacy of state revenues to provide increased demands for improved and new public services, and business and administrative attitudes toward the tax or fiscal climate all play a much more important role in state growth than state tax cost levels. Despite the negative effect that the degree of interindustry structural tax inequality of the BAT might have had on business location decisions, when the BAT is viewed in the context of its role in the overall fiscal system of Michigan, it can be judged as having had a net favorable effect on the state's development.

11

Summary of Findings

The fiscal and political circumstances leading to the enactment of the BAT included a chronic revenue–expenditure gap and executive and legislative battles between proponents and opponents of a corporate net income tax. In order to break a political stalemate, the BAT was introduced in the last days of the 1953 Michigan legislative session as a substitute for the net income tax proposal. The BAT was adopted in 1953 as a temporary tax, more because of opposition to a business net income levy than on its own merits. In 1955 it was made a permanent part of the Michigan revenue structure until its replacement in 1968 with an individual and corporate net income package.

The BAT base was computed by subtracting from gross receipts all outlays, with certain exceptions, which were treated under the IRS code as ordinary and necessary expenses of conducting business. These deductions included cost of merchandise purchases, supplies, utilities, insurance, advertising fees, rent and interest paid, and an allowance for depreciation of real property. The deductability of these items was justified on the basis that they were interfirm purchases, that is, amounts paid which were included in the adjusted receipts of the selling enterprise and therefore taxed at an earlier stage of production. For example, wages, salaries, and all other compensations to employees, distributions to partners, and dividends paid to stockholders were not deductible because they did not qualify as purchases from other firms. The BAT base was broader than that of a profits levy, but narrower than that of a gross income tax. Essentially, the tax base approximated the economist's concept of value added, the sum of income originating in business enterprise. Furthermore, it was defined as applicable to all legal forms and industrial types of business, extending from the agricultural and extractive industries to service trades and retailing.

Rationale

Since the BAT was a broad-based levy which applied to Michigan business activity regardless of level of profitability, it was consistent with the conceptual justification for subnational taxing of business enterprise: employing the business enterprise as a tax collecting intermediary is the only procedure for taxing individuals, wherever they may reside, for the benefits of public services accruing initially to the business enterprise. It follows that the services of government should be treated as a factor of production similar to the services of land, labor, capital, and entrepreneurship, and that their costs should be incorporated into the pricing structure.

Revenue Productivity

Throughout its existence the BAT was an important revenue factor for Michigan. Despite its low statutory rate, the tax was consistently the second largest source of state General Fund revenues, second only to the retail sales tax. An examination of the change in the BAT collections relative to changes in Michigan personal income also indicates that the tax was more than proportionately responsive to economic growth; as a result, it introduced an important element of income elasticity into the existing unresponsive Michigan revenue structure. On the other hand, the BAT was less responsive to changes in economic activity (that is, state personal income) than business net income tax measures. Although this characteristic would argue for a net income tax in periods of state economic expansion, the relative income inelasticity of the BAT would be desirable in times of economic recession.

Tax Impact

Although the BAT was defined as a broad-based tax on all sizes and organizational forms of business, the bulk of the revenue was collected from large corporations. An examination of the *de facto* BAT coverage of total gross receipts of business taxpayers indicates that this impact was due to the practical effect of the combined minimum standard deduction and the specific dollar exemption provisions. Although many small unincorporated businesses were excluded from the scope of the tax, they accounted for less than 5 percent of total receipts generated by Michigan business. In terms of the BAT's coverage of the total dollar value generated, the objective of comprehensiveness of coverage, which was claimed by the original BAT proponents as a merit of the tax, was achieved.

Structural Distribution

The BAT, through specific statutory provisions, achieved its intended objective of comprehensive coverage of the business value generated within the tax jurisdiction, but it did so in a manner which was structurally discriminatory among various industry groups. In terms of both business tax burden and tax cost measures, the BAT exhibited an uneven distribution pattern of tax liabilities. In contrast, both a net income and a value-added levy exhibited an evenness of distribution. To the extent that this structural tax inequality violated the equity or neutrality principle in business taxation and was a negative influence on business decisions to locate within a state, the 1967 Michigan legislature had the option of one of two policy approaches. It either could modify the BAT to make its structure correspond to that of a value-added tax, or could replace the BAT with an individual (for noncorporate business) and corporate net income levy. The net income levy was the choice.

Neutrality

In the context of the objectives of state business tax policy, *neutrality* refers to the effect of taxes on the allocation of resources. In particular, it implies a minimization of interference with private economic decisions regarding input mix and type of business organization which would be made in the absence of the tax. Within this framework, the BAT violated two general criteria of neutrality: not all business organizations were taxed (financial institutions were exempt), and the tax did not apply to all factor input payments.

Regarding this latter point, three important loopholes existed. First, investment was treated inconsistently. The BAT permitted a statutory deduction for the depreciation of real property assets, but disallowed a deduction for other capital costs. Second, there was a dual rate structure: public utilities were given a preferential rate *vis-à-vis* other industrial groups. Third, property incomes were treated unequally; interest and dividends received were excluded from gross receipts, but only interest paid was an allowable statutory deduction in computing the tax base. The net result was to ignore the practical similarity of these payments regarding the problem of attracting capital, and thus to discriminate between equity financing in favor of debt financing in much the same manner as a net income tax.

Economic Effects

The economic nature of the BAT's adjusted receipts base relative to business tax shifting in an open or subnational economy meant that probably as much as 60 percent of the total BAT liability was shifted forward to consumers, in the form of higher prices, and the remainder was shifted backward to factor suppliers. To the extent that the tax was shifted forward by manufacturers, nearly 80 percent of it was exported, or paid by non-Michigan residents. This evidence supports the argument by various writers that the certainty of tax shifting of the BAT ranks above the net income tax, which replaced the BAT.

When the BAT was examined for its effect on business location and/or expansion decisions, it was noted that its interindustry structural tax inequality might have a negative effect on those decisions. However, in the context of this and other factors which affect location choices, such as revenue adequacy, neutrality among inputs *vis-à-vis* alternative levies, height of tax rate, and tax rationale, the BAT can be counted as having had a net favorable effect, if any.

Administration and Compliance

Administrators and business executives alike claimed that the BAT met the objectives of certainty and simplicity in administration and of ease of taxpayer compliance. For administrators, the practical effect of the deduction and specific dollar exemption provisions was to reduce the number of returns requiring auditing; for the taxpayer, the BAT return could be made directly from income statement data.

Interstate Receipts

The interindustry tax liability effects of four alternative formulas have been proposed both at the state and federal level as mandatory methods for the division of a multistate firm's total tax base. Estimates made from BAT tax returns indicate that for a state such as Michigan, in which manufacturers operating in multistate export-orientated business constitute a large part of the industrial tax base, the inclusion of an origin property and/or a payroll factor in the determination of taxable receipts is essential if the tax is to meet revenue productivity criteria at reasonably low statutory rates.

Conclusion

Throughout the life of the BAT, proponents of a conventional business net income levy attempted to modify the BAT in order to incorporate considerations of ability to pay, or profitability, into the statute. On the other hand, supporters of the tax argued that amendments could be made to make it more nearly conform to the structure of a value-added (net income variant) tax. Finally, in the 1967 Michigan legislative session the net income tax proponents succeeded in replacing the BAT with a profits levy.

This replacement had positive and negative trade-offs. Increased income responsiveness and a reduction in the discriminatory nature of the structural tax liability distribution (tax cost and burden measures) were advantages gained. They were realized at the cost of such merits as a low statutory tax rate, consistency with the benefits received justification for state business taxation, and, relative to the profits tax, certainty of tax shifting and neutrality among factor inputs. Most of the merits of the BAT could have been retained and the structural tax defects (for example, structural tax distribution patterns and neutrality among types of capital and property incomes) eliminated, or at least reduced, had those who had supported modification of the BAT to a value-added tax prevailed. Although the BAT itself did not conform to the structure of a value-added tax, its defects argue for that form.

For various reasons the Michigan attempt at a comprehensive and conceptually rational form of taxation on business enterprise was replaced with the more conventional levy. In conclusion, it is appropriate to ask whether, in light of the BAT experience, other subnational governments will succeed in introducing new principles and rationale into business tax policy, or whether they also will revert to traditionally accepted practices.

Appendix A

Sample BAT Return

Sample BAT Return

A sample annual BAT return is presented below. The first part of the return is a general summary and computation of the tax due; Schedules A through H serve as worksheets. The reader will note that although the taxpayer was legally required to compute his unapportioned adjusted receipts tax base by the subtraction method (Schedule B), this figure could also have been determined by an addition method (sum of lines 27, 28, 29, and 31 of Schedule C).

REVISED 1964
B.A. 10
State of Michigan

DEPT. OF
REVENUE

Calendar Year

-----------------DO NOT WRITE ABOVE THIS LINE--------------------

BUSINESS ACTIVITIES TAX - ANNUAL RETURN

OR FISCAL YEAR

Beginning __July 1__ 19 _66_
Ending __June 30__ 19 _67_

Individual
Partnership
Michigan Corporation __X__
Foreign Corporation
Other

Check One

A HYPOTHETICAL B.A.T. RETURN

0000000

Nedrif Manufacturing Company
1217 Grand River Blvd.
Milan, Michigan 48000

RETURN IS DUE → __12/31/67__

	ACCOUNT NUMBER	T. K.	COUNTY	CITY	FILE DATE
	0000000	13	00		7/67

PLEASE COMPLETE FULLY — If the name of owner or partners' names are not part of the above address or it is incorrect in any other way, please show below the complete owner(s) name, trade name and address.

Name of Owner(s)____ Nedrif, Inc. ____

Federal Employers Identification Number____ 12-345678 ____

Social Security Number____

Trade Name____ Nedrif Manufacturing Co. ____

Address____ 1217 Grand River Blvd., Milan ____ ZIP CODE __48000__

Occupation or type of business__ Manufacturer of office equipment __

DID YOU FILE FOR LAST YEAR? __X__ YES____ NO

If this is your first return show date business was started____

If return covers less than a full year show period covered FROM____ TO____

If this is a final return show name of successor(s)____

COMPUTATION - SEE INSTRUCTIONS

1. Taxable balance (from page 3)..$ 2,649,368
*2. Tentative tax at 7-¾ mills (.00775)...20,533
3. Less net income credit (line 2 above) $ 20,533 x 4.93 % (line 32-page 2) 1,027
4. Tax 19,506
5. Less amounts paid with declaration, quarterly or tentative returns ....$ 14,800
    Add any overpayment on previous year's tax not refunded.............................$
6. If your tax (line 4) is larger than payments (line 5) enter the balance due here....................
7. If your tax (line 4) is less than payments (line 5) enter overpayment here
    ....OVERPAYMENT $
    Check whether overpayment be ( ) Refunded to you; ( ) Credited on your next quarterly return.
8. Penalty Plus interest if filed after due date (of amount on line 6)
    Penalty 5% per month or fraction thereof to a maximum of 25%...................$
    PLUS interest at the rate of 1% per month ....$

9. Total tax, penalty and interest...TO BE PAID WITH THIS RETURN. ⟶ $ 4,706
* Taxpayers qualifying as public utilities use 2 mills (.002).

I declare under the penalties imposed by Act No. 150, P. A. 1953 As Amended, that this return, including any accompanying schedules and statements, has been examined by me and to the best of my knowledge and belief is a true, correct and complete return.

Return prepared by   J. R. Kamaaina   Signed_____
    Office of Treasurer
Address   Nedrif Mfg. Co. Milan   Title___President

Make all remittances payable to **State of Michigan**
    and mail to:
    MICHIGAN DEPARTMENT OF REVENUE
    200 TUSSING BUILDING
    LANSING, MICHIGAN 48922

State whether individual owner, member of firm, executor, administrator, trustee, etc. or give title if officer of a corporation.

Reviewed_____Calculated_____

11

PAGE 2

SCHEDULE A - EXCLUSIONS FROM TOTAL GROSS RECEIPTS

1. Total Gross Receipts...$ 62,600,900
    Less: (a) Sales of capital assets...$ 555,000
    (b) Amounts received as an agent solely on behalf of another.......................... -0-
    (c) Refunds on returned merchandise.. 109,600
    (d) Cash discounts allowed.. 124,999
    (e) Other Interest and dividends   113,037
                 Explain
    Total Exclusions...$ 902,636
2. Gross receipts for tax purposes (Carry to line 1-Schedule D or F)..$ 61,698,264

SCHEDULE B - ALLOWABLE BUSINESS DEDUCTIONS - SEE INSTRUCTIONS

3. Inventory beginning of period...$ 11,143,300
4. Merchandise purchased for manufacturing or resale....................... 30,655,413
5. Total 41,798,713
6. Less inventory end of period.. 7,327,559

7. Cost of goods sold... 34,471,154

8. Rent paid (Business expense only).. 710,788
9. Interest paid on business indebtedness... 69,026
10. Taxes (Do not deduct federal excise and sales tax unless
    they are included in reported gross)... 877,500
11. Depreciation (From Schedule E)... 271,250
12. Repairs (Do not include capitalized improvements)... 500,990
13. Power, Heat, Light and Water.. 1,358,205
14. Freight 21,985
15. Postage, telephone and telegraph.. 359,041
16. Advertising 1,263,746
17. Insurance 500,099
18. Supplies 837,300
19. Travel expense 892,866
20. Dues to business associations.. 50,000
21. Other Bad debts   200,150
22. Other Charitable contributions   39,363
23. Other Legal and professional fees   856,123
24. Other Miscellaneous (e.g., payment to exempt trust)   1,065,343
25. Total allowable deductions (Add lines 7 through 24)..$ 44,469,348
26. Difference (Subtract line 25 from line 2 and complete lines 2 and 3 of Schedule D or Schedule F) 17,228,916

SCHEDULE C - DETERMINATION OF NET INCOME CREDIT PERCENTAGE

27. Salaries and wages (do not include amounts paid to proprietor or partners) .... $ 13,338,894
28. Personal property depreciation .... $ 346,297
29. State and city income taxes.. $ 50,000
30. Total of lines 27 thru 29 (Subtract this amount from line 26).. $ 13,735,191
    (If line 30 is equal to or greater than line 26, see instructions)
31. Net income for year for credit computation.. $ 3,493,725

32. Computation of net income credit percentage $___172,298___ divided by $___3,493,725___ = ___4.93___ %
                                1% of line 3   line 31   Not to Exceed 25%
                                page 3

PAGE 3

SCHEDULE D - TO BE COMPLETED BY TAXPAYERS WITH MICHIGAN RECEIPTS ONLY

1. Gross receipts for tax purposes (From line 2-Schedule A)... $
2. Less allowable deductions - use the greater of (1) 50% of line 1 above;
   (2) line 25-Schedule B (page 2); or (3) line 6-Schedule G (page 4) ....
3. Adjusted receipts for computation of tax - line 1, less line 2. ....
4. Less statutory exemption ($12,500 for full year or $1,041.66 per month) ....
5. Taxable balance - Carry to line 1-page 1 ....

SCHEDULE E
ALLOWANCE FOR DEPRECIATION ON REAL PROPERTY ONLY

To be Prepared by those Taxpayers Claiming Depreciation on Schedule B, Line 11.
(Do Not Claim Depreciation on Furniture, Fixtures, Equipment or any Other Tangible Personal Property).

1. Kind of Real Property	2 Date acquired	3. Cost or other basis	4. Depreciation allowed (or allowable) in prior years	5. Method of computing depreciation	6. Rate (%) or life (years)	7. Depreciation for this year
1. Buildings-- (warehouse)	-- 10/10/42	$	$			$ -- 81,251
2. Factory	11/27/42					190,000

Total (to be shown as Line 11-Schedule B-Page 2)... $ 271,250

Total Depreciation Per Federal Return (Real & Personal)...................................... $ 617,547
(Attach additional schedules if necessary)

SCHEDULE F - TO BE COMPLETED BY TAXPAYERS WITH RECEIPTS FROM MICHIGAN AND OTHER STATES

1. Gross receipts for tax purposes (From line 2-Schedule A).. $ 61,698,264
2. Less allowable deductions - use the greater of (1) 50% of line 1 above;   44,469,348
   (2) line 25-Schedule B (page 2); or (3) line 6-Schedule G (page 4)........................
3. Adjusted receipts for computation of tax - line 1, less line 2. 17,228,916
4. Allocation percentage (From page 4-Schedule H)... 15.45%
5. Allocated adjusted receipts (Multiply line 3 by allocation percentage)....(Mich. A.R. base)........... 2,661,868
6. Less statutory exemption ($12,500 for full year or $1,041.66 per month)............................. 12,500
7. Taxable balance - Carry to line 1-page 1. 2,648,368

SCHEDULE G

To be used only by taxpayers whose allowable deductions are less than 50% of reported gross receipts but whose payroll exceeds 50% of reported gross receipts.

1. Gross receipts for tax purposes (from line 2-page 2) ....$_____
2. Deduction (50% of gross receipts)...
3. Annual payroll ...._____
4. Payroll excess (line 3 less line 2).._____
5. 50% of line 4– or 10% of line 1 whichever is the lesser amount...._____
6. Total allowable deductions. Add lines 2 and 5 and forward to line 2-page 3 ....$_____

DOES NOT APPLY

$_____

SCHEDULE H

To be used only by those taxpayers doing business in Michigan and one or more other states or foreign countries.

Taxpayers other than those deriving receipts from the rendition of transportation services as specified in Sub-section (c) of Section 3 of Act No. 150, P. A. 1953, As Amended, will use the percentage determined in this schedule in the computation of tax on Page 3.

Determination of allocation percentage

*PART 1—(A)	Property within Michigan .... $	3,852,560	
(B)	Total property	27,826,051	
(C)	Percentage (Divide property within Michigan by total property)...		13.85 %
PART 2—(D)	Payroll Within Michigan............................ $	2,237,656	
(E)	Total payroll	13,338,893	
(F)	Percentage (Divide payroll within Michigan by total payroll)		16.71 %
**PART 3—(G)	Sales with Michigan destination................. $	9,699,199	
(H)	Total sales	61,368,277	
(I)	Percentage (Divide sales with Michigan destination by total sales)		15.80 %
PART 4—(J)	Total percentage (Total of percentages shown in C, F, I)................................		46.36 %
PART 5—(K)	Allocation percentage (J divided by 3. Carry resulting percentage to line 4-Schedule F-page 3)...		15.45 %

*Rental expenditures for the use of real property are to be multiplied by 8 and the resulting product included in the property factors.
**Sales include sales of merchandise, services rendered, income from rents and royalties and all other business receipts.

Taxpayers deriving receipts from the rendition of transportation services as specified in Sub-section (c) of Section 3 of Act No. 150, P. A. 1953, As Amended, determine the allocation percentage to be shown on page 3, by showing details of such computation below.

In the case of a taxpayer authorized under the statute to use one of the special formulae, use the lines provided below and explain:

(a) Numerator.._____
(b) Denominator..._____

Divide numerator by denominator to obtain percentage to be allocated to Michigan.
Percentage taxable..............._____% (Carry to line 4-Schedule F-page 3)

Appendix B

Summary of the
Legislative History

Summary of the

Legislative History

Except as noted, chapter 2 on statutory provisions describes the BAT at the time of its repeal in 1968. The following is a synopsis of major legislative actions and amendments to the tax from 1953–1968.

1953 Enactment

The legislature enacted the Business Activities Tax, effective 1 July 1953 to 15 March 1955. Its features included: (1) a tax base of adjusted receipts (gross receipts less certain allowable deductions, with a specific exemption of $10,000 per taxpayer); and (2) tax rates of 1 mill for utilities and 4 mills for all other business subject to the levy.

1954 Amendments

These amendments were largely of an administrative character. The more significant changes were an addition of specific allocation formulas for multistate pipelines; extension for filing time of annual returns; provision to every taxpayer of the option to omit quarterly returns by paying annually in advance; and authorization for affiliated firms to file consolidated returns.

1955 Amendments

Act 150, P.A. 1953, as amended by Act 285, P.A. 1955, was effective as of 1 July 1955. (1) The tax rate was increased to 1.5 mills for utilities and 6.5 mills for other business. (2) Depreciation and amortization on real property was allowed. Prior to this, no depreciation, amortization, or depletion allowances were permitted. (3) Supplementary excess payroll deduction was permitted. (4) The income allocation formula for multistate business was changed from a sales factor index to a three-factor equal weight formula of payroll, real and tangible personal property, and sales.

1959 Amendments

Act 262, Laws 1959, increased tax rates to 2 mills for utilities and to 7¾ mills for other business, enacted the net income credit provision, and increased the specific dollar exemption from $10,000 to $12,500 per taxpayer.

1961 Amendments

Act 89, Laws 1961, made various administrative changes regarding the due date of annual returns, refunds, and late filing penalties. In addition, royalty income from intangible personal property no longer was exempt from the tax.

1967 Repeal

Act 281, Laws 1967, repealed the BAT, effective 1 January 1968.

Appendix C

Data Sources and
Construction of Estimates

Data Sources and

Construction of Estimates

The purpose of this appendix is to indicate data sources and methods of estimate construction used in this book. Discussion of the conceptual limitations of the data is confined to those aspects not already noted in the text. Part I is a description of the sources employed; Part II specifically discusses the various estimates used in the chapters.

Part I: General Data Sources

The three general sources for data in this study were national (U.S.) data, Michigan secondary sources, and Michigan primary sources.

National Sources

U.S. COMMERCE AND TREASURY DEPARTMENT. State and local tax analysis is handicapped by the lack of estimates of relevant subnational data. Periodic statistics are available for state expenditures and revenues, but there are none on the size of the various tax bases by state. However, the U.S. Department of Commerce publishes some information which can be used in construction of state estimates. For example, state personal income components by states are published annually by the U.S. Department of Commerce, Office of Business Economics, *Survey of Current Business* (Washington, D.C.: U.S. Government Printing Office). The listing of the publication of this type of state information can be found in the following: U.S. Department of Commerce, Bureau of the Census, *Directory of Federal Statistics for States, 1967* (Washington, D.C.: U.S. Government

Printing Office, 1968), and in the annual December index of the *Survey of Current Business*.

The U.S. Department of the Treasury publishes state business income account and balance sheet data for unincorporated businesses. This information is found in "Business Income Tax Returns" published annually in U.S. Department of Treasury, Internal Revenue Service, *Statistics of Income* (Washington, D.C.: U.S. Government Printing Office). This data is available for states because the U.S. Internal Revenue code taxes noncorporate business through the separate returns of owners.

Corporations, the bulk of which operate in multistate activities, are permitted to file from the home office (common parent corporation) state, and, as a result, no apportionment of business income statement items is made to the various states. Consequently, the corporate component of state business tax base data for those taxes not actually employed by a state jurisdiction must be indirectly estimated. Total U.S. corporation data for 1965 is published in U.S. Department of Treasury, Internal Revenue Service, *Statistics of Income — 1965, Corporation Income Tax Returns* (Washington, D.C.: U.S. Government Printing Office, 1969).

ACIR. The Advisory Commission on Intergovernmental Relations periodically publishes reports on budgetary aspects of state governments. Two commission reports which were used for tax base estimates and revenue data were: ACIR, *Measures of State and Local Fiscal Capacity and Tax Efforts*, Report M-16 (1962), and *State and Local Finances, Significant Features 1966 to 1969*, Report M-43 (1968) (Washington, D.C.: U.S. Government Printing Office). The first report presents estimates of alternative total state tax bases (for example, corporation net income), and the second is a compilation of state revenue (and expenditure) magnitudes and effort.

NPA. The Center for Economic Projections of the National Planning Association publishes a range of state economic statistics. Of these, the most useful for a tax study such as this one are statistics on state gross product originating by major industrial sectors: National Planning Association, Center for Economic Projections, *State Projections to 1975*, Report No. 65-II (Washington, D.C.: the Association, 1965).

Secondary Michigan Sources

Four publications were of particular use for this study: Michigan Department of Treasury, Revenue Division, *Annual Report* (Lansing: Michigan Department of Treasury, 1953–1968); Daniel B. Suits and Research Seminar in Quantitative Economics, *An Econometric Model of Michigan*, Technical Report No. 3 (Lansing: Michigan Department of Commerce, 1966); Harvey E. Brazer, Marjorie C. Brazer, Cynthia S. Cross, and Michael Zweig, *General Fund Estimates of Revenue and Expenditures to 1975*, Technical Report No. 11 (Lansing: Michigan Department of Commerce, 1967); and John L. Hazard, *Michigan's Commerce: Domestic and International*, Technical Report No. 5 (Lansing: Michigan Department of Commerce, 1966).

Technical Report No. 3 presents estimates of Michigan gross state product (GSP) from 1949–1963 for manufacturing; mining; contract construction; wholesale and retail trade; services; finance, insurance, and real estate; transportation; communication; public utilities; agriculture; and government. Technical Report No. 11 updated GSP data through 1965. Michigan GSP measures the total dollar volume of productive activity carried on within Michigan as is conceptually described in chapter 4 in the text. Michigan GSP estimates were greater than the gross product originating (GPO) figures of the National Planning Association, whose estimates were constructed by summing individual industrial activities after national industrial projections were allocated among the fifty states. The NPA estimates involved various arbitrary determinations and assumptions of state industrial mix which were modified in the Michigan Department of Commerce reports to explicitly take into account the influence of various national factors on the state's economy. Consequently, the Michigan GSP estimates were, unless otherwise noted, employed in making tax base and structural tax cost estimates for this study.

Primary Michigan Data

The major primary source was made available through permission of the Michigan Revenue Division of the Department of Treasury to examine data from the 1965 Business Activities Tax returns. In June 1969 the Revenue Division pulled all returns having more than $5,000 in tax liability; twenty-eight items from each tax return were transcribed. The BAT return numbers for type of business classification of the various taxpayers were based on an industry classification system unique to Michigan. Although the state classifications were similar to those defined in U.S. Bureau of the Budget, Office of Statistical Standards, *Standard Industrial Classification Manual* (Washington, D.C.: U.S. Government Printing Office, 1967), they were not identical. The first step in organizing the BAT return data, identification of each of the firms by SIC code, was a detailed task. It was accomplished by using both the information from the "Occupation or type of business" line on page 1 of the BAT return, and by making a cross-reference for each of the returns reviewed with Moody's Investor Service, *Moody's Industrial Manual: American and Foreign* (New York: Moody's, Inc., 1965 and 1966).

The criteria for coding industries for SIC purposes were those listed in the *Standard Industrial Classification Manual*, Appendix D. For example, identification of the manufacturing classification was based on the major activity of the taxpayer as determined by the value of production statistics in *Moody's* and by the description on the BAT return itself. The classification was made on a one-digit basis for the eight major industry groups which were defined as taxpayers under the BAT statute: agriculture; mining; construction; manufacturing; transportation, communications, and public utilities; wholesale trade; retail trade; and services. The finance, insurance, and real estate industry was specifically excluded from the BAT. Consequently, it is not presented in any of the data tables in the text of this study. A two-digit breakdown was done for manufacturing and service trades.

Once the tax return data was organized by its SIC code, the Michigan statistics to be used were computed by firm and by industry. Four examples follow.

1) *Value added*: Sum of rent paid, interest paid, net income, cost of labor, salaries and wages, compensation of officers, and other payroll.
2) *Value added including income taxes*: Sum of (1) plus income taxes paid to any government.
3) *Adjusted receipts, addition method*: Sum of salaries and wages (including payroll for officers), personal property depreciation, state and city income taxes paid, and net income.
4) *Modified adjusted receipts levies*: Sum of adjusted receipts plus real depreciation and depletion.

In addition, computations were made for the various types of tax base forms described in chapter 4. These figures were used to constantly cross-check estimates for use in the tables in the main text of this study. For example, item (1) above approximates the net income variant of value added. When this figure was used as the "value-added" base in the various tables for the differential impact analysis (chapter 7), estimates also were made for a gross product variant in order to check that the former figure quantitatively was consistently more "net" than the latter.

As noted, these figures were computed from the BAT returns, but it was not always possible to use this primary data. Accordingly, similar sums were computed on special worksheets from national and secondary Michigan sources. When using aggregate industry data, problems arose in computing the tax base to conform to various BAT or value-added definitions. As a result, it was necessary to devise methods to modify national data to Michigan circumstances. Two of these problems will be briefly discussed to give an idea of methodology.

Depreciation. The national sources cited above do not separate the real and personal property components of total depreciation, but this information was on the BAT returns. Whenever national sources were needed to indirectly estimate a BAT or modified BAT base, industry weighted averages from the Michigan returns were used.

Cost of Goods Sold. A taxpayer's cost of goods sold is an allowable deduction in the computation of adjusted receipts and value-added type taxes. No problems arose when using BAT returns or unincorporated Michigan business data from Internal Revenue Service sources; it was a matter of summing net inventory change (see chapter 4), materials and supplies expense, and merchandise purchased. However, when using IRS corporation data for indirect measurement of tax bases, the "cost of goods sold" item is included in a "cost of sales and operations" entry. Unlike noncorporate data, the "cost of sales and operations" entry includes a payroll item (direct cost of labor) which must be netted out of the BAT interfirm purchase deductions.

This difficulty was solved by computing a "cost of sales and operations" estimate for noncorporate business by industry type, and finding a ratio of the nonpayroll elements to the total figure. The ratio was then applied to the corporate "cost of sales and operations" figure. This approach makes an implicit assumption that the labor cost element of a "cost of sales and operations" entry is similar for noncorporate and corporate firms in a given industry. Despite this constraint the approach was necessary when IRS corporate data were used. Although BAT data did not include this separate "cost of labor" item, it was possible to use the tax returns to check these relationships by computing the payroll (schedule B, line 27 in Appendix A) to cost of goods sold (schedule B, line 7 in Appendix A) ratios for Michigan by industry. This cross-check showed consistency of the estimates.

Other national source items which were similarly modified to Michigan circumstances were amortization and depletion, business receipts (the treatment of royalties and rent received varied from the BAT), payroll (the treatment of officers' salaries, cost of labor), and profit (the distribution to partners and estimates of income taxes for value-added base purposes). The two main reference items used in these efforts were: Michigan Department of Treasury, Revenue Division, *Rules and Regulations of the Business Activities Tax*, Adm. Code R. 205.551 − R. 205.565, Act 150, P.A. 1953 As Amended (Lansing: the Department, 1967); and *Statistics of Income — 1965 Business Tax Returns*, "Law and Terminology" section, pp. 293 ff.

Use of National Data Sources

Use of national data often involved making an implicit assumption that the Michigan economy conforms to the national economic structure. Such an assumption might be quite reasonable in instances where Michigan produced a large share of certain national outputs (for example, durable manufacturing), but tenuous in other circumstances (for example, mining). However, the defects of the use of this data can be reduced by the use of Michigan primary and secondary sources to modify not only total industry tax base data, but also tax base components. The constant modification of national data (if used) to fit Michigan industrial circumstances was done throughout this study.

Part II: Construction of Various Estimates

Chapter 4

Estimates for Tables 3 and 4 were made as follows. Total business tax base data initially were computed from U.S. Department of Treasury, Internal Revenue Service, *Statistics of Income — Business Tax Returns: 1965*. Adjustments were made in various items as discussed above. The data further were modified to meet Michigan circumstances by an application of Michigan to national GSP and GSP component ratios from Michigan Department of Commerce sources. Resulting figures were checked for consistency with both National Planning Association gross product originating estimates by industry and state and BAT return figures. The primary data further were used to estimate real and personal property depreciation breakdowns by industry groups.

In order to conceptually approximate a business firm's or industry's value-added profits, that is, actual net operating profits, this item (Table 3, column 4) should exclude dividends received from other firms, and capital gains and losses, and should include the dollar value of the owner's consumption of the firm's products and taxes measured by income. Table 3 includes an estimate of income taxes based on relationships of lines 29 and 31 from the BAT return (net income for credit purposes, line 31, included federal taxes on or measured by net income and excluded gain or loss on disposition of capital assets). Therefore, Table 4 includes in the profits item an estimate of taxes imposed by any government on or measured by income plus any taxes not related to the business from which the gross receipts were derived.

Chapter 5

The methods of data collection and estimation for Tables 5 through 10 are discussed in the text and are indicated in the table source citations. As noted in the text, BAT elasticity estimates for Table 11 were based on figures adjusted for tax rate and base definitions consistent with 1965 statutes. The corporate profits tax base was estimated from IRS data and then modified for Michigan by reference to the corporation profits tax base computed for the state *vis-à-vis* the national economy published in ACIR, *Measures of State and Local Fiscal Capacity and Tax Effort*, Report M-16 (Washington, D.C.: U.S. Government Printing Office, 1962), chapter 3, especially pp. 48–49 and Table 10. Since the ACIR data were for 1960, the industry figures were grossed up to 1965 by using the projection rates of industrial economic activity in Michigan Department of Commerce technical reports 3 and 11. The total net income, gross receipts, and federal tax liability bases were constructed in the manner described for chapter 4. The Michigan personal income data used were taken from the April and August 1968 issues of the *Survey of Current Business*. Conceptual interpretations and limitations of the results and the choice of the time periods observed are discussed in the text.

Chapter 6

All data used in tables were from Michigan secondary sources.

Chapter 7

The construction of the various tax bases used in chapter 7 has been discussed on pages xxx–xxx of this appendix. All of the general data sources – national and primary and secondary Michigan sources – were used to compute numerators and denominators for the tax cost and burden measures. The procedure to determine industry dollar tax payments under various types of equal yield substitute business taxes was to divide the total tax yield (the 1965 BAT dollar yield was used) by the various tax base sizes. The effective equal yield tax rate, therefore, varied inversely with the tax base estimates. Because the Michigan tax jurisdiction, like that of any government, did not employ the range of taxes under examination, this tax payment estimation approach was necessary to get the desired measures of inter- and intraindustry structural tax inequality. It is the relative tax distribution patterns and industry positions (*vis-à-vis* other industries and various tax types) that is of interest in a differential impact analysis. If the, estimating methods described above are consistently applied, they can identify structural tax characteristics of substitute levies. Because the focus was on relative positions, the tax cost and burden ratios were divided by an all-industry weighted average to make comparisons easier. (See footnote 12, chapter 7 for the use of weighted rather than unweighted data.) Total manufacturing was broken down by reference to Michigan industry statistics of value added by manufacturers published in the U.S. Department of Commerce, Bureau of the Census, *Annual Survey of Manufacturers, 1964 and 1965* (Washington, D.C.: U.S. Department of Commerce, 1968), Table 3, pp. 243–45.

Chapter 8

The following worksheet was used to compute data for the various apportionment formulas for multistate business receipts.

Worksheet:
Alternative Apportionment
Formulas for Multistate Income,
1965

		One Factor	Two Factor	Three Factor	Accounts paying over $———— Weighted Formula
1	Property percentage	0	%	%	%
2	Payroll percentage	0	%	%	%
3	Sales percentage			0	%	%
4	Sum				
5	Allocation percentage	%	%	%	%
6	Adjusted receipts	$	$	$	$
7	Multiply by (5) percentage				
8	Apportioned adjusted receipts				
9	Less specific $ exemption	12,500	12,500	12,500	12,500
10	Taxable balance				
11	Tentative tax (#10 × .00775)				
12	Net income credit percentage	%	%	%	%
13	Net income credit (#11 × #12)	$	$	$	$
14	Tax due (#11 less #13)	$	$	$	$

Data used were from the BAT returns. Tax due data for each tax return and by all four apportionment approaches were computed. Those firms which previously had been classified for SIC purposes were put in their industry groups and industry tax due sums were computed. This was done both for all BAT returns made available by the Michigan Revenue

Division and for accounts paying over $50,000. Not all two-digit manufacturers were listed in Tables 28 and 29 due to insufficient data, and no breakdown above $50,000 was published because such groups are dominated by a few large firms. To publish that data might have enabled identification of individual taxpayers, a violation of a disclosure agreement made with the state of Michigan.

Chapter 9

Data in Tables 30 and 31 were computed by procedures similar to those described above for the tables in chapter 7. The method used to arrive at minimum gross taxed estimates by industry type was presented in the text. In order to determine number of businesses by size of gross receipts, the data sources for Table 32 were national. This was necessary because such a breakdown, for noncorporate as well as corporate business, was not available for states. Similar problems which required a reliance on national sources when estimating revenue effects of various apportionment formulas by state were encountered by the Special Subcommittee on State Taxation of Interstate Commerce. Unlike the subcommittee's report, this book, in solving the estimating problem, did not use national sources in order to distribute property, payrolls, and sales among the states by industry; that Michigan data was available from the BAT returns. See *State Taxation of Interstate Commerce,* Report of the Special Subcommittee on State Taxation of Interstate Commerce, Committee on the Judiciary, U.S. House of Representatives, 88th Cong., 2d sess. (Washington, D.C.: U.S. Government Printing Office, 1964), pp. 534-37 and Appendix G.

The procedure for estimating the figures in Table 32 was to sum the percentage of number of firms and of gross receipts below the various minimum gross receipts levels which had been determined earlier (Table 30) by industry type for the BAT. In applying this method to Michigan two implicit assumptions are accepted: (1) the industry-by-industry distribution of receipts in Michigan is the same as for the national economy; and (2) the size distribution of receipts within Michigan industry groups conforms to the national economy distribution pattern. It is clear that such assumptions limit the extent to which conclusions may be drawn regarding the comprehensiveness of coverage of the BAT. Nonetheless, they are useful in presenting an idea of the coverage of the BAT adjusted receipts type levy, and of the revenue relationships between one apportionment formula and another.

Selected

Bibliography

Articles

Aaron, Henry. "What Is a Comprehensive Tax Base Anyway?" *National Tax Journal* 22 (December 1969): 543–49.

Bahl, Roy W., and Shellhammer, Kenneth L. "Evaluating the State Business Tax Structure: An Application of Input–Output Analysis." *National Tax Journal* 22 (June 1969): 203–16.

Barber, Arthur A. "A Suggested Shot at a Gordian Knot of Income Apportionment." *National Tax Journal* 13 (September 1960): 243–51.

Barnes, Donald K. "The Business Receipts Tax." *Michigan State Bar Journal* 32 (October 1953): 31–39.

Blank, David M. "The Role of the Real Property Tax in Municipal Finances." *National Tax Journal* 7 (December 1954): 319–23.

Boyle, Gerald J. "The Anatomy of Fiscal Imbalance." *National Tax Journal* 21 (December 1968): 412–24.

Brazer, Harvey E. "The Value of Industrial Property as a Subject of Taxation." *Journal of Canadian Public Administration* 55 (June 1961): 137–42.

Bronfenbrenner, M. "The Japanese Value-Added Sales Tax." *National Tax Journal* 3 (December 1950): 298–313.

Bronfenbrenner, M., and Kogiku, Kiichus. "The Aftermath of the Shoup Tax Reforms." Parts I and II. *National Tax Journal* 10 (September and December 1960): 236–54; 345–60.

Colm, Gerhard. "Conflicting Theories of Corporate Income Taxation." *Law and Contemporary Problems* 7 (Spring 1940): 281–90.

Cragg, John G.; Harberger, Arnold C.; and Mieszkowski, Peter. "Empirical Evidence on the Incidence of the Corporation Income Tax." *Journal of Political Economy* 75 (December 1967): 811–21.

Dickerson, Milton B. "The New Business Receipts Tax." *Business Topics* (East Lansing, Michigan) 1 (November 1953): 1–7.

Due, John F. "Studies of State–Local Tax Influences on Location of Industry." *National Tax Journal* 14 (June 1961): 168–73.

————. "The Value Added Tax." *Western Economic Journal* 3 (Spring 1965): 165–71.

Earlyham, G. W. "Politics Stymies State Finance Crisis." *Inside Michigan*, May 1953, pp. 15–19.

Forte, Francesco. "On the Feasibility of a Truly General Value Added Tax: Some Reflections on the French Experience." *National Tax Journal* 19 (December 1966): 337–61.

Groves, Harold M. "Neutrality in Taxation." *National Tax Journal* 1 (March 1948): 18–24.

Groves, Harold M., and Kahn, C. Harry. "The Stability of State and Local Tax Yields." *American Economic Review* 42 (March 1952): 87–102.

Harriss, C. Lowell. "Economic Aspects of Interstate Apportionment of Business Income." *Taxes* 37 (April 1959): 327–28.

————. "Interstate Apportionment of Business Income." *American Economic Review* 49 (June 1959): 398–401.

King, Donald A., and Lefkowitz, Martin. "The Finances of State and Local Governments." *Survey of Current Business*, October 1967, pp. 20–31.

Kinnear, George. "The Multistate Tax Commission: A New Experiment in Intergovernmental Relations." *Canadian Tax Journal* 19 (March-April 1971): 136–43.

Landers, Frank. "Michigan's Business Activities Tax." *State Government* 27 (October 1954): 210–15.

Legler, John B., and Papke, James A. "Optimizing State Business Taxation: An Application of Differential Impact Analysis." *National Tax Journal* 18 (September 1965): 240–46.

Legler, John B., and Shapiro, Perry. "The Responsiveness of State Tax Revenue to Economic Growth." *National Tax Journal* 21 (March 1968): 46–56.

Lindholm, Richard W. "A Plea for the Value Added Tax." *Tax Review* 30 (May 1969): 17–24.

————. "The Value Added Tax: A Short Review of the Literature." *Journal of Economic Literature* 8 (December 1970): 1178–89.

Lock, Clarence W.; Rau, Donovan J.; and Hamilton, Howard D. "The Michigan Value Added Tax." *National Tax Journal* 8 (December 1955): 357–71.

Lynn, Arthur D., Jr. "The Uniform Division of Income for Tax Purposes Act Re-Examined." *Virginia Law Review* 66 (October 1960): 1257–68.

McLure, Charles E., Jr. "Commodity Tax Incidence in Open Economies." *National Tax Journal* 17 (June 1964): 187–204.

————. "The Interstate Exporting of State and Local Taxes: Estimates for 1962." *National Tax Journal* 20 (March 1967): 49–77.

Mieszkowski, Peter. "The Incidence Theory: The Effects of Taxes on the Distribution of Income." *Journal of Economic Literature* 7 (December 1969): 1103–24.

Mueller, Eva, and Morgan, James N. "Location Decisions of Manufacturers." *American Economic Review, Papers and Proceedings* 52 (1962): 206–17.

Oakland, W. H. "The Theory of the Value Added Tax: Comparison of Tax Bases." *National Tax Journal* 20 (June and September 1967): 119–36; 270–81.

Papke, James A. "Michigan's Value Added Tax after Seven Years." *National Tax Journal* 13 (December 1960): 350–63.

Pogue, Thomas F., and Sgontz, L. G. "Value Added vs. Property Taxation of Business: Effects on Industrial Location." *Land Economics* 58 (May 1971): 150–57.

Sagendorph, Kent. "Truth about the New State Tax — It's Fair — Plays No Favorites." *Inside Michigan*, July 1953, pp. 18–19.

Schmidt, E. B. "Determining Structural Tax Inequalities among Business Firms." *Nebraska Journal of Economics and Business* 2 (Spring 1962): 29–39.

Shoup, Carl S. "Consumption Tax, and Wages Type and Consumption Type of Value Added Tax." *National Tax Journal* 21 (June 1968): 153–61.

Siedman, L. William. "Something New in Taxation." *Michigan Business Review* 6 (1954): 23–28.

Studenski, Paul. "Toward a Theory of Business Taxation." *Journal of Political Economy* 68 (October 1940): 621–54.

Waldorf, W. H. "The Responsiveness of Federal Personal Income Taxes to Income Change." *Survey of Current Business*, December 1967, pp. 32–45.

Weinrobe, Maurice D. "Corporate Taxes and the United States Balance of Trade." *National Tax Journal* 24 (March 1971): 79–86.

Books and Proceedings

Adams, Thomas S. "The Taxation of Business." In *Proceedings of the Eleventh Annual Conference on Taxation*, pp. 185–94. New York: National Tax Association, 1917.

Anderson, Theodore A. "Recommended Changes in Michigan's Tax Structure." In *Taxes and Economic Growth in Michigan*, edited by Paul W. McCracken, pp. 17–24. Kalamazoo: Upjohn Institute for Employment Research, 1960.

Back, Kenneth. "The Rodino Bill — The Heart of the Matter." In *Proceedings of the Sixty-Second Annual Conference on Taxation*, pp. 604–12. Columbus: National Tax Association, 1969.

Bahl, Roy W., and Shellhammer, Kenneth L. "Fiscal Planning and State Business Taxation: An Application of Input–Output Analysis." In *Proceedings of the Sixty-First Annual Conference on Taxation*, pp. 418–

32. Columbus: National Tax Association, 1968.

Barnes, Donald K. "The Anomalous Michigan Business Activities Tax." In *Proceedings of the Sixty-First Annual Conference on Taxation*, pp. 115–17. Columbus: National Tax Association, 1968.

Beaman, Walter H. *Paying Taxes to Other States*. New York: Ronald Press, 1963.

Bonser, Charles F.; Kiesling, Herbert J.; Patterson, D. Jeanne; and Swartz, Thomas R. *Business Taxation in Indiana*. Indianapolis: Bureau of Business Research, Indiana University, 1966.

Brazer, Harvey E., ed. *Michigan Tax Study Staff Papers*. Lansing: Legislative Committee, House of Representatives, 1958.

—————. *Taxation in Michigan: An Appraisal*. Ann Arbor: University of Michigan Institute of Public Administration, 1961.

Buehler, Alfred G. "The State and Local Tax Structure and Economic Development." In *Taxes and Economic Growth in Michigan*, edited by Paul W. McCracken, pp. 25–56. Kalamazoo: Upjohn Institute for Employment Research, 1960.

Cline, Denzel C., and Taylor, Milton C. *Michigan Tax Reform*. East Lansing: Michigan State University Institute for Community Services, 1966.

Colm, Gerhard, and Helzner, Manuel. "Financial Needs and Resources over the Next Decade." In *Public Finances: Needs, Sources, and Utilization*. A Conference Report of the National Bureau of Economic Research, pp. 3–21. Princeton: Princeton University Press, 1961.

Commerce Clearing House. *Michigan Tax Reports*, pp. 6551–669. Chicago: Commerce Clearing House, 1967.

Coughlan, J. D., and Strand, W. K. *Depreciation: Accounting, Taxes, and Business Decisions*. New York: Ronald Press, 1969.

Due, John F. *Government Finance: Economics of the Public Sector*. 4th ed. Homewood: Richard D. Irwin, Inc., 1968.

—————. "Reform of the Michigan Tax Structure." In *Taxes and Economic Growth in Michigan*, edited by Paul W. McCracken, pp. 57–68. Kalamazoo: Upjohn Institute for Employment Research, 1960.

—————. *Sales Taxation*. Urbana: University of Illinois Press, 1957.

—————. "Value Added Tax Proposals in the United States." In *Public Finance and Welfare: Essays in Honor of C. Ward Macy*, edited by Paul L. Kleinsorge, pp. 111–26. Eugene: University of Oregon Press, 1966.

Ebel, Robert D. "The Michigan Business Activities (Value Added) Tax: A Retrospective Analysis and Evaluation." In *Proceedings of the Sixty-First Annual Conference on Taxation*, pp. 90–107. Columbus: National Tax Association, 1968.

Ebel, Robert D., and Papke, James A. "A Closer Look at the Value Added Tax." In *Proceedings of the Sixtieth Annual Conference on Taxation*, pp. 155–70. Columbus: National Tax Association, 1967.

Ecker-Racz, L. L. "Emerging Fiscal Issues: Roundup of the Seminar." In *Proceedings of the Seminar on Balancing Our Federal-State-Local Fiscal System*, pp. 421–22. Columbus: National Tax Association, 1971.

Eldridge, Douglas H. "Equity, Administration and Compliance, and Intergovernmental Fiscal Aspects." In *The Role of Direct and Indirect Taxes in the Federal Revenue System,* pp. 141–204. Princeton: Princeton University Press, 1964.

Firmin, Peter A. *The Michigan Business Receipts Tax.* Ann Arbor: University of Michigan Press, 1953.

Friedlaender, Ann F. "Incidence and Price Effects of Value Added Taxes." In *Proceedings of the Sixty-Fourth Annual Conference on Taxation.* Columbus: National Tax Association, forthcoming.

Goode, Richard. *The Corporation Income Tax.* New York: John Wiley & Sons, 1951.

Gornick, Alan. *The Michigan Business Receipts Tax – Its Basis and Economic Theory.* Ann Arbor: University of Michigan Law Institute, 1952.

Greenhut, Melvin L. *Plant Location in Theory and Practice.* Chapel Hill: University of North Carolina Press, 1956.

Groves, Harold M. "Michigan Taxes and Economic Growth." In *Taxes and Economic Growth in Michigan,* edited by Paul W. McCracken, pp. 85–98. Kalamazoo: Upjohn Institute for Employment Research, 1960.

Harriss, C. Lowell. "Income Apportionment among the States: A Sales Factor Does Not Belong in the Formula." In *Seminar on the Taxation of Interstate Business,* pp. 63–68. New York: Tax Foundation, Inc., 1970.

Hellerstein, Jerome R. "State Taxation of Interstate Business: Reflections on Legislative Directions." In *A Symposium on Federal-State-Local Fiscal Relationships,* pp. 257–67. Princeton: Tax Institute of America, 1968.

Herber, Bernard P. *Modern Public Finance.* Rev. ed. Homewood: Richard D. Irwin, Inc., 1971.

Hicks, Ursula. *Public Finance.* New York: Pitman Co., 1947.

Hirsch, Werner Z. *The Economics of State and Local Government.* New York: McGraw-Hill, 1970.

Huber, William; McKean, Eugene C.; and Taylor, Harold C. *The Michigan Economy.* Kalamazoo: Upjohn Institute for Employment Research, 1959.

Johnston, Kenneth Stanton. *Corporation's Federal Income Tax Compliance Costs.* Columbus: Ohio State Bureau of Business Research, 1963.

Karaska, Gerald J., and Bramhall, David F., eds. *Locational Analysis for Manufacturing.* Cambridge, Mass.: The M.I.T. Press, 1969.

Kauper, Paul G., and Estep, Samuel D. "Interstate Transactions Covered by the Tax." In *A Syllabus of the Presentations on the New Business Receipts Tax,* pp. 11–20. Ann Arbor: University of Michigan Law Institute, July 1953.

Krzyzaniak, Marian, ed. *Effects of the Corporation Income Tax.* Detroit: Wayne State University Press, 1966.

Krzyzaniak, Marian, and Musgrave, Richard A. *The Shifting of the Corporation Income Tax.* Baltimore: Johns Hopkins Press, 1963.

Legler, John B., and Papke, James A. "Toward a Rationalization of State–Local Business Taxation." In *Proceedings of the Fifty-Eighth Annual Conference on Taxation,* pp. 541–51. Columbus: National Tax Association, 1965.

Lewis, Wilfred, Jr. *Federal Fiscal Policy in the Postwar Recessions.* Washington, D.C.: The Brookings Institution, 1965.

Lindholm, Richard W. "The Business Activities Tax." In *Michigan Tax Study Staff Papers,* pp. 263–67. Lansing: Legislative Committee, House of Representatives, 1958.

————. "Integrating a Federal Value Added Tax with State and Local Sales Levies." In *Proceedings of the Seminar on Balancing Our Federal-State-Local Fiscal System,* pp. 403–11. Columbus: National Tax Association, 1971.

Lock, Clarence W. "Administrative History of Michigan's Business Activities Tax." In *Proceedings of the Forty-Eighth Annual Conference on Taxation,* pp. 20–25. Columbus: National Tax Association, 1955.

————. "An Administrator's Point of View of the Value Added Tax." In *Alternatives to Present Federal Taxes,* pp. 55–63. Princeton: Tax Institute of America, 1964.

Mattersdorf, Leo. "Suggested Changes in Michigan's Tax Structure." In *Taxes and Economic Growth in Michigan,* edited by Paul W. McCracken, pp. 141–47. Kalamazoo: Upjohn Institute for Employment Research, 1960.

Maxwell, James A. *Financing State and Local Government.* Rev. ed. Washington, D.C.: The Brookings Institution, 1969.

McClure, Charles E., Jr. "The Value Added Tax and State and Local Finance." In *Proceedings of the Sixty-Fourth Annual Conference on Taxation.* Columbus: National Tax Association, forthcoming.

McCracken, Paul W., ed. *Taxes and Economic Growth in Michigan.* Kalamazoo: Upjohn Institute for Employment Research, 1960.

Musgrave, Richard A., ed. *Essays in Fiscal Federalism.* Washington, D.C.: The Brookings Institution, 1965.

————. *The Theory of Public Finance.* New York: McGraw-Hill, 1959.

Musgrave, Richard A., and Daicoff, Darwin W. "Who Pays Michigan Taxes?" In *Michigan Tax Study Staff Papers,* pp. 161–82. Lansing: Legislative Committee, House of Representatives, 1958.

National Bureau of Economic Research. *Public Finances: Needs, Sources, and Utilization.* A Conference Report of the National Bureau of Economic Research. Princeton: Princeton University Press, 1961.

National Bureau of Economic Research and the Brookings Institution. *The Role of Direct and Indirect Taxes in the Federal Revenue System.* Princeton: Princeton University Press, 1964.

Netzer, Dick. *Economics of the Property Tax.* Washington, D.C.: The Brookings Institution, 1966.

Oldman, Oliver. "Taxation of Interstate Business." In *Proceedings of the Sixty-Second Annual Conference on Taxation,* pp. 619-25. Columbus: National Tax Association, 1969.

Papke, James A. "Research and State Tax Reform." In *Proceedings of the Fifty-Sixth Annual Conference on Taxation,* pp. 366–70. Columbus: National Tax Association, 1963.

————. "The Taxation of Business Enterprise: Some Unsettled Issues." In *Proceedings of the Fifty-Fourth Annual Conference on Taxation,* pp. 559–69. Columbus: National Tax Association, 1961.

Phares, Donald. "Equity in State–Local Taxation: An Interstate Analysis." In *Proceedings of the Sixty-Fourth Annual Conference on Taxation*. Columbus: National Tax Association, forthcoming.

Preston, Howard M. "The Michigan Business Activities Tax as Viewed by Operators of Small Establishments." In *Proceedings of the Forty-Eighth Annual Conference on Taxation*, pp. 34–35. Columbus: National Tax Association, 1955.

Ratliff, Charles E., Jr. *Interstate Apportionment of Business Income for Tax Purposes*. Chapel Hill: University of North Carolina Press, 1962.

Rafuse, Robert W., Jr. "Cyclical Behavior of State–Local Finances." In *Essays in Fiscal Federalism*, edited by Richard A. Musgrave, pp. 63–121. Washington, D.C.: The Brookings Institution, 1965.

Sanden, B. Kenneth. "The Value Added Tax: Its Application and Practice." In *Proceedings of the Sixty-Fourth Annual Conference on Taxation*. Columbus: National Tax Association, forthcoming.

Shoup, Carl S. "Suggested Changes in the State and Local Tax System of Michigan." In *Taxes and Economic Growth in Michigan*, edited by Paul W. McCracken, pp. 148–67. Kalamazoo: Upjohn Institute for Employment Research, 1960.

——————. *Public Finance*. Chicago: Aldine Press, 1969.

——————. "Theory and Background of the Value Added Tax." In *Proceedings of the Forty-Eighth Annual Conference on Taxation*, pp. 7–19. Columbus: National Tax Association, 1955.

Slitor, Richard E. "The Role of Value Added Taxation in the Tax Structure of the States: Prospective Developments." In *Proceedings of the Sixty-First Annual Conference on Taxation*, pp. 107–15. Columbus: National Tax Association, 1968.

Stapchinskas, J. P. "Taxation of Business in Michigan: Viewpoints of Businessmen." In *Proceedings of the Forty-Eighth Annual Conference on Taxation*, pp. 25–27. Columbus: National Tax Association, 1955.

Stephenson, E. C. "The Michigan Business Activities Tax: A Retailer's Viewpoint." In *Proceedings of the Forty-Eighth Annual Conference on Taxation*, pp. 29–33. Columbus: National Tax Association, 1955.

Sullivan, Clara K. *The Tax on Value Added*. New York: Columbia University Press, 1965.

Tax Foundation. *Current Problems and Issues in State Taxation of Interstate Commerce*. Government Finance Brief No. 3. New York: the Foundation, 1966.

——————. *Taxation of Interstate Business*. A Tax Foundation Seminar. New York: the Foundation, 1970.

Tax Institute. *How Should Corporations Be Taxed?* New York: the Institute, 1946.

——————. *Reappraisal of Business Taxation*. Princeton: the Institute, 1962.

Tax Institute of America. *Alternatives to Present Federal Taxes*. Princeton: the Institute, 1964.

——————. *Federal-State-Local Fiscal Relationships*. Princeton: the Institute, 1968.

Public Documents

Advisory Commission on Intergovernmental Relations. *Fiscal Balance in the American Federal System.* Vol. 1. Washington, D.C.: U.S. Government Printing Office, 1967.

⸺. *State and Local Finances: Significant Failures 1966 to 1969.* Report M-43. Washington, D.C.: U.S. Government Printing Office, 1968.

⸺. *Sources of Increased Tax Collections: Economic Growth Versus Political Choice.* Washington, D.C.: U.S. Government Printing Office, 1968.

⸺. *State-Local Taxation and Industrial Location.* Washington, D.C.: U.S. Government Printing Office, 1967.

⸺. *Tax Overlapping in the United States – 1964.* Washington, D.C.: U.S. Government Printing Office, 1964.

Brazer, Harvey E.; Brazer, Marjorie C.; Cross Cynthia S.; and Zweig, Michael. *General Fund Estimates of Revenue and Expenditures to 1975.* Technical Report No. 11. Lansing: Michigan Department of Commerce, State Resource Planning Program, 1967.

Bronder, Leonard D., and Koval, John M. *Michigan's Future: Its Population and Economy.* Technical Report No. 10B. Lansing: Michigan Department of Commerce, State Resource Planning Program, 1967.

Citizens Advisory Group. *Michigan Tax Survey, 1952.* A Report to the Legislative Interim Tax and Revenue Study Committee. Detroit: the Group, 1952.

Hazard, John L. *Michigan's Commerce: Domestic and International.* Technical Report No. 5. Lansing: Michigan Department of Commerce, State Resource Planning Program, 1966.

Michigan Department of Treasury, Revenue Division. *Annual Report.* Lansing: the Department, 1953–1969.

⸺. *Business Activities Tax Rules.* Lansing: 1965 and 1967.

⸺. *Michigan Business Activities Tax, Act 150.* Public Acts of 1953 as Amended, 1967.

National Planning Association, Center for Economic Projections. *State Projections in 1975.* Washington, D.C.: the Association, 1965.

Suits, Daniel B., and Research Seminar in Quantitative Economics. *Econometric Model of Michigan.* Technical Report No. 3. Lansing: Michigan Department of Commerce, State Resource Planning Program, 1966.

U.S., Congress, House, Special Subcommittee on State Taxation of Interstate Commerce, Committee on the Judiciary. *State Taxation of Interstate Commerce.* 88th Cong., 2d sess. Washington, D.C.: U.S. Government Printing Office, 1964.

U.S. Department of Commerce, Bureau of the Census. *Annual Survey of Manufacturers.* Washington, D.C.: U.S. Government Printing Office, 1964 and 1965.

⸺. *Compendium of Government Finances.* Washington, D.C.: U.S. Government Printing Office, 1953–1967.

_____. *Historical Statistics on Governmental Finances and Employment.* Washington, D.C.: U.S. Government Printing Office, 1967.

U.S. Department of Treasury, Internal Revenue Service. *Statistics of Income: 1965 Business Income Tax Returns.* Washington, D.C.: U.S. Government Printing Office, 1968.

_____. *Statistics of Income: 1965 Corporation Income Tax Returns.* Washington, D.C.: U.S. Government Printing Office, 1969.

University of Wisconsin Tax Study Committee. *Wisconsin's State and Local Tax Burden.* Madison: University of Wisconsin Press, 1959.